Social Issues
in Literature

Wildness in
Jack London's
The Call of the Wild

Other Books in the Social Issues in Literature Series:

Class Conflict in Emily Brontë's *Wuthering Heights*

Colonialism in Joseph Conrad's *Heart of Darkness*

Death and Dying in the Poetry of Emily Dickinson

The Environment in Rachel Carson's *Silent Spring*

Family Dysfunction in Tennessee Williams's *The Glass Menagerie*

Poverty in John Steinbeck's *The Pearl*

Race in Ralph Ellison's *Invisible Man*

Sexuality in William Shakespeare's *A Midsummer Night's Dream*

Teen Issues in S.E. Hinton's *The Outsiders*

Violence in Anthony Burgess's *A Clockwork Orange*

War in Ernest Hemingway's *A Farewell to Arms*

War in Kurt Vonnegut's *Slaughterhouse-Five*

Women's Issues in Margaret Atwood's *The Handmaid's Tale*

Social Issues
in Literature

Wildness in Jack London's *The Call of the Wild*

Gary Wiener, Book Editor

GREENHAVEN PRESS
A part of Gale, Cengage Learning

GALE
CENGAGE Learning·

Farmington Hills, Mich • San Francisco • New York • Waterville, Maine
Meriden, Conn • Mason, Ohio • Chicago

Elizabeth Des Chenes, *Director, Content Strategy*
Cynthia Sanner, *Publisher*
Douglas Dentino, *Manager, New Product*

For more information, contact:
Greenhaven Press
27500 Drake Rd.
Farmington Hills, MI 48331-3535
Or you can visit our Internet site at gale.cengage.com

For product information and technology assistance, contact us at

Gale Customer Support, 1-800-877-4253
For permission to use material from this text or product, submit all requests online at www.cengage.com/permissions

Further permissions questions can be emailed to permissionrequest@cengage.com

Articles in Greenhaven Press anthologies are often edited for length to meet page requirements. In addition, original titles of these works are changed to clearly present the main thesis and to explicitly indicate the author's opinion. Every effort is made to ensure that Greenhaven Press accurately reflects the original intent of the authors. Every effort has been made to trace the owners of copyrighted material.

Cover image © Everett Collection Inc./Alamy.

LIBRARY OF CONGRESS CATALOGING-IN-PUBLICATION DATA

Wildness in Jack London's The call of the wild / Gary Wiener, book editor.
    pages cm. -- (Social Issues in Literature)
Includes bibliographical references and index.
ISBN 978-0-7377-6992-0 (hardcover) -- ISBN 978-0-7377-6993-7 (pbk.)
1. London, Jack, 1876-1916. Call of the wild. 2. Nature in literature. 3. Animals in literature. 4. Human-animal relationships in literature. I. Wiener, Gary.
PS3523.O46C3938 2014
813'.52--dc23
                                                                2013036417

Printed in the United States of America
1 2 3 4 5   18 17 16 15 14

Contents

Introduction   9

Chronology   18

Chapter 1: Background on Jack London

1. The Life of Jack London   23

   Daniel Dyer

   Jack London sought out adventure throughout his life. His trip to the Yukon during the gold rush gave him material for the stories that would make him famous.

2. London's Love of the Wild Had a Dark Side   34

   Charles Paul Freund

   Jack London is best known for his tales of the Yukon, but there is another side to his writing that shows a man who believed in white superiority and who wrote stories about ethnic genocide.

3. Jack London Was Not a Racist   42

   Dan Davidson and the Klondike Sun *Staff*

   The opinions of London's racist characters should not be confused with those of the author himself. London had a relatively enlightened attitude toward race.

4. London's Yukon Trip Changed His Life   46

   James L. Haley

   London's early struggles culminated in his trip to the Yukon, undertaken to strike it rich through gold mining. However, London found real treasure when a sudden realization ignited his writing career.

Chapter 2: Wildness in *The Call of the Wild*

1. Jack London's Enduring Appeal   54

   Eric Miles Williamson

   Although Jack London's work has fallen out of favor with contemporary literary critics, his powerful works, which pit characters against a lonely, alienating, brutal world, deserve a better reception.

2. On Primitivism in *The Call of the Wild*   **63**
   Richard Fusco

   Contrary to those who claim that Buck's story ends with
   a descent into pure primitivism, London's canine hero
   instead finds in the wolf pack a new family that can offer
   him the freedom he desires.

3. Jack London's *The Call of the Wild*   **69**
   Raymond Benoit

   The Call of the Wild is London's paean to the pastoral
   world. Through Buck's story, it is clear that London prefers the simple, natural life over the complex and con-
   torted world of civilization.

4. Buck Takes a Mythical Journey
   into the Unknown   **75**
   Earle Labor and Jeanne Campbell Reesman

   Buck's metamorphosis from domestic canine to a larger-
   than-life deific creature is a mythical quest, in which
   readers can experience a version of their own deepest desires for selfhood.

5. Buck Escapes the Capitalist System
   by Returning to the Wild   **85**
   Gina M. Rossetti

   The Call of the Wild is a socialist folktale, in which Buck's
   return to the wild allows him to escape the degradation
   of forced labor.

6. *The Call of the Wild* Is a Study in Devolution   **94**
   Jacqueline Tavernier-Courbin

   In order to survive in his harsh new environment, Buck
   must leave behind the ways of civilized domesticity and
   devolve into an amoral creature concerned only with fulfilling his own needs.

7. Jack London: The Problem of Form   **102**
   Donald Pizer

   The Call of the Wild is a fable that appeals to readers' unconscious longing for freedom and simplicity in a world
   where power becomes destiny.

8. *The Call of the Wild* Pits Society   109
Against Wildness
Charles N. Watson Jr.

In its depiction of the protagonist escaping from civilization into the wild, *The Call of the Wild* shares themes
and motifs with two other great American novels: *The
Adventures of Huckleberry Finn* and *Moby-Dick*.

9. London's Animal Depictions Are Deceptive   122
John Perry

To mesh with the prevailing philosophy of naturalism,
London made his animals into men in furs, rather than
accurately depicting how real wolves acted in their natural environment.

10. London's Essay "Husky: The Wolf-Dog of the   130
North" Offers Insights into His Dog Novels
S.K. Robisch

In an early essay, when his Yukon experiences were
fresh in his memory, London described the characteristics of the dogs that would figure so prominently in his
life and in his writings.

11. London's Protagonists' Quests for Individualism   140
Are Paradoxical
Paul Deane

London's protagonists, such as Buck, strive to escape
the boundaries of civilized society and become self-
sufficient individuals. However, this individuality comes
at a high price.

Chapter 3: Contemporary Perspectives on Wildness

1. Out of the Wilderness   150
Jerry Adler

Studies show that fewer people are getting out into the
wild. However, it may be time to give nature a chance
to recover from what hordes of tourists have done to
the most famous spots in the natural world.

2. Modern Attitudes Toward Wolves   154
   in the Wild Vary Greatly
   Economist

   Wolves in Europe and America were almost exterminated. Modern conservation efforts have led to their
   comeback, but not everyone is happy about the resur-
   gence of the wolf population.

3. A Woman Needs a Wild Side   166
   Suzanne Paola

   While not proud of a past that includes drug use and
   dropping out of high school, a poet and professor asserts
   that having a wild side can provide necessary balance for
   achieving a fulfilling life.

4. Wildness Inspires Freedom and Integrity   172
   bell hooks

   A well-known African American writer celebrates her
   Kentucky Appalachian upbringing and the wildness that
   it instilled in her life. She still draws on this wildness
   many years after having moved away.

For Further Discussion   177

For Further Reading   179

Bibliography   181

Index   187

Introduction

In his book of essays *The Practice of the Wild*, American nature poet Gary Snyder meditates on the evolution of the terms "wild and free":

> An American dream-phrase loosing images: a long-maned stallion racing across the grasslands, a V of Canada geese high and honking, a squirrel chattering and leaping limb to limb overhead in an oak. It also sounds like a Harley Davidson. Both words, profoundly political and sensitive as they are, have become consumer baubles.[1]

Snyder adds, "To be truly free one must take on the basic conditions as they are—painful, impermanent, open, imperfect—and then be grateful for impermanence and the freedom it grants us."[2]

In his fiction as well as in his life, Jack London continually sought out the wild and the free, and, like Snyder, he was to accept the good and the bad when it came to the untamed world. At fifteen years of age, the future author was already breaking the law as an oyster pirate off the coast of California. By the age of seventeen, he sailed to Japan and the North Pacific with a seal-hunting expedition. At eighteen, he tramped across the United States, even serving a thirty-day prison term for vagrancy in Niagara Falls. At twenty-one, he joined the Klondike gold rush, enduring unimaginable hardships in the frozen north and living, despite a bout with scurvy, to write about it in the books that would ensure his lasting fame.

Even after his books made him a household name and assured he could live on easy street, London was never satisfied with civilized life. With his second wife, Charmian, London embarked on an ambitious seven-year, around-the-world voyage on a forty-foot boat he had built especially for the journey. The trip was clearly quixotic and even foolhardy: The vessel needed major repairs at its first port in Hawaii, and London was forced to abandon the voyage within two years. However, the cruise of the *Snark* suggests that London was always seeking, in his life and in his art, a return to a simpler world away from the complications of society. As one of his premiere critics Earle Labor writes, "his career might well be studied as a lifelong series of attempts to escape the corruptions of civilization and to recapture the simpler maternal security of Nature."[3]

In his art as well, London was continually dragging his characters away from the ease of civilization into a strange, and often harsh, primitive world. In *The Sea Wolf*, for example, effete literary sophisticate Humphrey Van Weyden finds himself aboard a ship captained by the maniacal Wolf Larsen and must confront his inability to live in the brutal, unforgiving world of a seal-hunting expedition. Surprisingly, Van Weyden ultimately succeeds in adapting to Larsen's world. In *Martin Eden*, the autobiographical eponymous protagonist, overcoming one failure after another, finally succeeds in winning over the literary world and becoming a famous and wealthy author. Nevertheless, he rejects his newfound status, diving overboard from a ship and drowning himself in the ocean.

Similarly, in London's rarely read fable about the boxing world, *The Abysmal Brute*, protagonist Pat Glendon, a natural-born athlete and undefeated prizefighter, learns the ways of civilization only to reject them, refusing to fall prey to the corruption of the pugilistic world. At the end of the novel, he takes his wife and soul mate, Maud Sangster, a latter-day Eve, back to the Edenic world of his upbringing:

> Where a jagged peak of rock thrust above the vast virgin forest, reclined a man and a woman. . . . The trees were monotonously huge. Towering hundreds of feet into the air, they ran from eight to ten and twelve feet in diameter. Many were much larger. All morning they had toiled up the divide

through this unbroken forest, and this peak of rock had been the first spot where they could get out of the forest in order to see the forest.[4]

Theirs is an intimidating journey back to primeval nature.

In *The Call of the Wild*, Buck is stolen away from his peaceful alpha-dog existence on Judge Miller's farm and thrust into an inhospitable world, where surprisingly, he eventually excels. Buck has much to learn, or as London would have it, unlearn. He must cast off civilized behavior and enter the world of the primitive. The novel's epigraph, foreshadowing this descent of dog, is from John Myers O'Hara's poem, "Atavism," and reads:

> Old longings nomadic leap,
>
> Chafing at custom's chain;
>
> Again from its brumal sleep
>
> Wakens the ferine strain.[5]

The two unfamiliar words in the stanza, "brumal" and "ferine," call attention to themselves and suggest the theme of London's novel: Brumal is "wintery," and not just so; it refers to an extreme, the shortest day of the year. "Ferine" derives from "feral," or wild, and can suggest savagery, ferociousness, and brutality, the qualities long dormant in Buck that he must recapture to become a Klondike alpha dog, and ultimately, the mythical ghost dog of the story's ending. It is not surprising that following the epigraph, the next thing that the reader comes upon is the title of chapter one, "Into the Primitive."

With the opening of this chapter, London plays a bit of a game with readers who may have blindly approached *The Call of the Wild*:

> Buck did not read the newspapers, or he would have known that trouble was brewing, not alone for himself, but for every tidewater dog, strong of muscle and with warm, long hair, from Puget Sound to San Diego.[6]

To the uninitiated, the novel's opening suggests that Buck is a human. It is not until the phrase "every tidewater dog" that the reader realizes otherwise. After all, most novels are about people and not canines. But London continually conflates man and his best friend in *The Call of the Wild*, and for good reason. The literary phenomenon of naturalism was a dominant force in American letters during London's time. Naturalist novels, such as those of the Frenchman Émile Zola and Americans Frank Norris and Stephen Crane, depicted human affairs with stark realism, suggesting that people were products of environment and heredity, that these factors determined the course of one's life, and that humanity should be studied with scientific detachment. In such a deterministic universe, where free will may be only an illusion, human survival instincts are often little different from those of animals. According to Donna M. Campbell, "The conflict in naturalistic novels is often 'man against nature' or 'man against himself' as characters struggle to retain a 'veneer of civilization' despite external pressures that threaten to release the 'brute within.'"[7]

Thus Buck, thrown into the primitive by a series of unfortunate events, must hark to the ways of his wolfish ancestors and learn the law of club and fang in order to survive. At varying intervals, London depicts Buck hearing the call of his ancestors and reverting back to a more atavistic state. Like a human casting off his civilized ways to adapt to the wild, in the chapter "The Law of Club and Fang," Buck learns to be a less "dainty eater,"[8] to steal food, and to nestle deep into the snow in order to sleep comfortably. Once snuggled into his snow bed, he feels momentarily trapped: "The snow walls pressed him on every side, and a great surge of fear swept through him—the fear of the wild thing for the trap." But London sees this as a positive and natural expression of the resurfacing of his ancestral past: "It was a token that he was harking back through his own life to the lives his forebears; for he was a civilized dog, an unduly civilized dog, and of his own experience knew no trap and so could not of himself fear it."[9] The word "unduly" is important here. Meaning "excessively," "inappropriately," or "unjustifiably," London's diction suggests that Buck's natural state is the wild and that his life with Judge Miller was the anomaly. As London writes near the end of the chapter, Buck's "development (or retrogression) was rapid."[10] Then London connects Buck's current experiences with those of his forerunners:

> And not only did he learn by experience, but instincts long dead became alive again. The domesticated generations fell from him. In vague ways he remembered back to the youth of the breed, to the time the wild dogs ranged in packs through the primeval forest and killed their meat as they ran it down.[11]

Over the course of the next five chapters, Buck plunges deeper into his own past, as London explores a type of "collective unconscious" that psychiatrist Carl Jung would write about only a few years later: "And when, on the still cold nights [Buck] pointed his nose at a star and howled long and wolflike, it was his ancestors, dead and dust, pointing nose at star and howling down through the centuries and through him."[12]

In the third chapter, "The Dominant Primordial Beast," Buck's transformation into the leader of the pack is completed. He defeats the former head dog, Spitz, in a gruesome battle that concludes with a pack of huskies devouring the defeated foe. For London, as for Lord Alfred Tennyson, nature is "red in tooth and claw," and there is no mercy for the defeated. Here we see the influence of Englishmen such as Herbert Spencer, Thomas Huxley, and Charles Darwin, writers in whose work London was well versed. The concepts of survival of the fittest and natural selection come into play as London depicts Buck, stronger and craftier than his antagonist by virtue of heredity and environment, ascending to the top of the husky pecking order. In his story "The White Silence," London made his Darwinian interests explicit as men battle their own huskies for a dwindling food supply: "the hoary game of natural selection was played out with all the ruthlessness of its primeval environment," London states, as a man and woman fight off the huskies with axe and rifle butt.[13]

Just before the climactic battle between Buck and Spitz, London writes, "There is an ecstasy that marks the summit of life, and beyond which life cannot rise. And such is the paradox of living, this ecstasy comes when one is most alive, and it comes as a complete forgetfulness that one is alive."[14] Then London makes one of the book's central notions explicit, comparing Buck to himself as artist: "This ecstasy, this forgetfulness of living, comes to the artist, caught up and out of himself in a sheet of flame."[15] London's own connection with his lead dog, his sense that the artist, too, is freest when he allows himself to run wild, is made explicit. As Abraham Rothberg observes, "Not only was *The Call of the Wild* an allegory, it was a kind of autobiography as well. London's close identification with the wolf and the dog, in his life and in his books, is everywhere evident."[16] It is no secret that London's own trip to the Yukon had ended in failure, with the young prospector ill and nearly broke. According to biographer James L. Haley, London returned from the northland with but $4.50 in gold dust.[17] But a great metamorphosis was set into motion on the trip: London decided to become a writer. Throughout his life, London, the writer and the man, identified with the wolf, the very icon that Buck would become at the end of the story. He asked his friends to call him "Wolf" and signed his letters with that name; his projected mansion was to be called "Wolf House." The protagonist of *The Sea-Wolf*, a tortured, strikingly powerful autodidact (like London himself), was dubbed "Wolf Larsen." Rothberg writes, "London was not only telling the story of Buck's life, but of his own, demonstrating the principles of success and survival he had learned."[18]

Buck's own metamorphosis into a wolf dog, continues once he has defeated Spitz and becomes lead dog. In one of the book's strangest—and most atavistic—scenes, Buck lies by the campfire at night dreaming of an ancient world inhabited by a "hairy man" who sleeps in a fetal position by a similar fire, needed to ward off "many gleaming coals, two by two, which [Buck] knew to be the eyes of great beasts of prey." In this primitive world, man and beast are joined together even more closely than in the contemporary Yukon, the hairiness of the man and his bent posture ("He did not stand erect, but with trunk inclined forward from the hips . . .") aligning him with the beasts within and without.[19] As Jacqueline Tavernier-Courbin writes, "London accepted the animal basis of human existence, and even reveled in it."[20]

Once the call of the wild enters Buck's consciousness, it cannot be turned off. Even as he is at his most content since leaving the southland under the care of John Thornton, he cannot evade the siren song that lures him back to his essence:

> He was older than the days he had seen and the breaths he had drawn. He linked the past with the present, and the eternity behind him throbbed through him in a mighty rhythm to which he swayed as the tides and the seasons swayed.[21]

And later, London writes that the call has become so strong "that each day mankind and the claims of mankind slipped farther from him":

> Deep in the forest a call was sounding, and as often as he heard this call, mysteriously thrilling and luring, he felt compelled to turn his back upon the fire and the beaten earth around it, and to plunge into the forest, and on and on, he knew not where or why.[22]

John Thornton's death in chapter seven at the hands of the Yeehats frees Buck completely, allowing him to fulfill the destiny that London had set out for his protagonist from the minute Buck was kidnapped by Manuel. It is a tale of devolution, a story of getting back to nature in the truest sense, in a way no human can hope fully to do. When Mark Twain had his character Huck Finn light out for the territory, Huck knew that he had to stay "ahead of the rest," because others would surely follow. Ernest Hemingway, London's adventure writing heir, often sent protagonist and alter ego Nick Adams into the woods to escape the complexities of modern civilization and the troubling decisions that accompany living in such a world. But the real world always draws such characters back in. Adams may get a respite, but often, as in stories such as "Big Two-Hearted River" and "The Three Day Blow," civilization is waiting with all of its problems and complications for the moment when the protagonist emerges from the wild.

However, London's choice to make his protagonist canine circumvents the issue of the return. Buck enters the world of myth, becoming the ghost dog to the Yeehats and the stuff of legend. His cubs symbolize his full immersion into the natural world, with no hint of the roar of Harley Davidsons to undermine the finality of London's message.

The viewpoints that follow explore further the nature of wildness in Jack London's writings and compare *The Call of the Wild* to London's other books, particularly its companion piece *White Fang*. They demonstrate why London's novel, while relegated to the ranks of young adult fiction by some critics, is still the most widely read American novel in the world.[23]

Notes

1. Gary Snyder, *The Practice of the Wild*. San Francisco, CA: North Point Press, 1990, p. 5.

2. Ibid.

3. Earle Labor, *Jack London*. New York: Twayne, 1974, p. 126.

4. Jack London, *The Abysmal Brute*. Lincoln: University of Nebraska Press, 2000.

5. John Myers O'Hara, "Atavism," *The Bookman*, November 1902, p. 226.

6. Jack London, *The Call of the Wild*. New York: Penguin, 1986, p. 43.

7. Donna M. Campbell, "Naturalism in American Literature," *Literary Movements*, Department of English, Washington State University. http://public.wsu.edu /˜campbelld/amlit/natural.htm.

8. Jack London, *The Call of the Wild*. New York: Penguin, 1986. p. 62.

9. Ibid, p. 59.

10. Ibid, p. 63.

11. Ibid, p. 64.

12. Ibid, p. 64.

13. Jack London, *Young Wolf: The Early Adventure Stories of Jack London*. Santa Barbara, CA: Capra, 1984, p. 77.

14. Jack London, *The Call of the Wild*. New York: Penguin, 1986, pp. 76–7.

15. Ibid, p. 77.

16. Abraham Rothberg, "Introduction," *The Call of the Wild and White Fang*. New York: Bantam Books, 1981, p. 7.

17. James L. Haley, *Wolf: The Lives of Jack London*. New York: Basic, 2010, p. 113.

18. Abraham Rothberg, "Introduction," *The Call of the Wild and White Fang*. New York: Bantam Books, 1981, pp. 7–8.

19. Jack London, *The Call of the Wild*. New York: Penguin, 1986. pp. 86–7.

20. Jacqueline Tavernier-Courbin, "*The Call of the Wild* and *The Jungle*: Jack London's and Upton Sinclair's Animal and Human Jungles," *The Cambridge Companion to American Realism and Naturalism*. Ed. Donald Pizer. New York: Cambridge University Press, 1995.

21. Jack London, *The Call of the Wild*. New York: Penguin, 1986, pp. 110–11.

22. Ibid, p. 111.

23. Jacqueline Tavernier-Courbin, *The Call of the Wild: A Naturalistic Romance*. New York: Twayne, 1994, p. 20.

Chronology

1876
Jack London is born on January 12 in San Francisco, California, to Flora Wellman and William Henry Chaney. Chaney abandons mother and son, and on September 7, Flora marries John London.

1878
London's family moves to Oakland, California.

1881
London's family moves to a farm in Alameda, California.

1886
The family buys a house in Oakland.

1891
London works in a cannery after finishing eighth grade. He becomes an oyster pirate.

1892
London joins the Fish Patrol, which catches oyster pirates.

1893
London sails on a seal-hunting schooner to the North Pacific. His experiences lead to the publication of his first story, "Typhoon Off the Coast of Japan."

1894
London works shoveling coal in a power plant in Oakland. He joins Coxey's Army, a group marching to Washington, DC, to protest the country's problematic economic situation.

1895
London attends Oakland High School.

1896

London leaves high school, studies for the entrance exam to the University of California, and attends college at the University of California at Berkeley for one semester before dropping out.

1897

With his brother-in-law, London joins the Klondike gold rush, sailing for Alaska. His quest is fruitless, and he decides to become a writer.

1898

London returns to California.

1899

London publishes stories, essays, and poems.

1900

London marries Elizabeth "Bessie" Maddern. He publishes the short story collection *The Son of the Wolf.*

1901

London's daughter, Joan, is born on January 15.

1902

London spends six months in the East End of London researching poverty for his book *The People of the Abyss.* The Londons' second daughter, Becky, is born.

1903

The People of the Abyss and *The Call of the Wild* are published. London separates from his wife.

1904

The Sea-Wolf is published.

1905

London marries Charmian Kittredge.

1906

London publishes *White Fang.*

1907

London begins his famous sea voyage on the *Snark,* first stopping in Hawaii. The trip is rife with problems. *The Road* is published.

1908

The *Snark* gets as far as Australia. London is hospitalized, ending the voyage at sea. *The Iron Heel* is published.

1909

London arrives back in California on August 29. He publishes *Martin Eden.*

1910

London makes plans for the construction of Wolf House, his elaborate mansion. A daughter, Joy, is born to the Londons, but she dies within two days.

1911

London publishes *The Cruise of the Snark* and *South Sea Tales.*

1912

London signs a five-year contract to write fiction for *Cosmopolitan* magazine. Work on Wolf House begins.

1913

London becomes the highest paid writer in the world. Just as Wolf House is finally nearing completion, it is destroyed by fire.

1914

London reports on the Mexican Revolution for *Collier's* magazine. He is forced to return home due to ill health.

1915

London publishes *The Star Rover*. He and Charmian spend five months in Hawaii.

1916

London dies on November 22. *The Little Lady of the Big House, The Turtles of Tasman,* and *The Acorn Planter: A California Forest Play* are published, as are numerous books in the years after his death.

Background on Jack London

The Life of Jack London

Daniel Dyer

Daniel Dyer is the author of Jack London: A Biography *and* Jack London's The Call of the Wild for Teachers.

In the following viewpoint, Dyer elaborates on the life of author Jack London. Born in San Francisco in 1876, London pursued his related interests in the sea and in adventure from an early age. As his alter ego, 'Frisco Kid, he even got himself thrown in jail for vagrancy in Niagara Falls, New York. When gold was found in the Canadian Yukon in 1897, London wasted little time in leaving for that wilderness, and his most famous tales, including The Call of the Wild, White Fang, *and the short story* "To Build a Fire," *stem from those adventures. With their publication, London became famous, and sales from his books enabled him to buy a yacht and a mansion. London's plans were ill-fated, however, as his home burned before he could move in and his sailing adventure brought on a variety of illnesses that may have contributed to his death at forty years of age.*

Jack London was a jailbird. A hobo. A sailor, seal hunter, pirate, gold miner, launderer, yachtsman, and coal shoveler. He was a drinker, a brawler, a heavy smoker. He was a husband (twice) and a father (twice). He was a socialist candidate for mayor of Oakland, California. He was a rancher. A world traveler. A voracious reader. A loyal correspondent whose collected letters fill three large volumes. A lecturer whose fiery speeches ignited controversy wherever he went. A journalist who covered wars and sporting events and natural catastrophes. He was an author of fifty books dealing with subjects as varied as sailing, boxing, out-of-body experiences, dogs, ranch-

Daniel Dyer, "Jack London (1876–1916)," *Writers for Young Adults.* Ed. Ted Hipple. vol. 2, 1E. Copyright © 1997 Cengage Learning.

ing, and Hawaii. He wrote about gold mining and animal rights, architecture and war, earthquake and fire, alcoholism and leprosy, surfing and socialism. He wrote one novel set in a prehistoric civilization, another set many centuries in the future. He wrote a murder mystery; he wrote a short novel about a devastating disease that wipes out nearly all human life. He wrote what may be the first "novelization" of a movie. He wrote about survival and love and loneliness, about fairness and unfairness, about right and wrong. He exhumed our past, examined our present, and predicted our future. And at the age of forty, he was dead.

Hobo and Prisoner

In 1894, 'Frisco Kid, age eighteen, was on the road, illegally sneaking aboard eastbound trains. He had left his home in Oakland, California, to join General Coxey's Industrial Army, a ragtag collection of people marching to Washington, D.C., to protest unemployment. "'Frisco Kid" was the youth's "monica" (moniker)—the nickname by which he was known to his fellow outlaw riders of the rails.

In Missouri, 'Frisco Kid and some companions—suffering from hunger and discouraged by the entire enterprise—deserted the army and returned to the trains, heading east. On 29 June, he was arrested in Niagara Falls, New York, by police who were rounding up the hundreds of homeless who had been, according to local newspapers, "flocking to this vicinity."

Unable to pay the twenty-five-dollar fine, 'Frisco Kid was sentenced to thirty days of hard labor in the Erie County Penitentiary, a dark, forbidding structure that housed about 800 inmates. They were serving sentences for crimes ranging from murder to rape to robbery to throwing snowballs. 'Frisco Kid's name appears on the roll of prisoners as John Lunden, occupation: sailor.

Released from the penitentiary, 'Frisco Kid eventually turned toward home, where he planned, at age nineteen, to enroll in high school. He had seen enough of the rough and unforgiving world he would later call "the abyss"—the pit of life.

A dozen years later (1907), 'Frisco Kid—now known to an admiring readership around the world as Jack London—published *The Road*, a collection of stories about his experiences as a hobo and prisoner. He accomplished in this volume, his nineteenth book, what he did in approximately fifty other works of fiction, nonfiction, and drama. By sheer effort, self-discipline, and talent he transformed what he called "raw life" into an enduring work of literary art.

London was part of a group of writers known as "realists" and "naturalists," the best known of whom were [American authors] Mark Twain, Edith Wharton, Henry James, Frank Norris, Stephen Crane, and Theodore Dreiser. These writers sought to create a popular literature that closely reflected real life, that involved characters struggling against the forces of nature and society. They wanted readers to recognize places and situations and problems similar to their own.

Many of London's tales take place in locations he knew intimately. In fact, the geography is often so precise that the movements of characters can be traced on a map. Some of his stories contain the names of actual historical figures—and of friends and family. Many of his characters face problems that he himself had faced.

Boyhood on the Bay

John Griffith London was born in San Francisco on 12 January 1876, to Flora Wellman. She always insisted that her son's father was William Chaney, an astrologer to whom she briefly had been married. Chaney, however, denied being the father and promptly abandoned Flora. Because she had difficulty nursing her little boy (called John Chaney at this time), Flora employed a wet nurse (a woman to breast-feed her child). She was Jennie Prentiss, an African American who maintained a lifelong friendship with Jack London.

In September 1876, Flora married a man fifteen years older than she, John London, forty-five, who by a previous marriage had eleven children, most of whom he had been forced by poverty to place in orphanages.

Throughout Jack London's boyhood, his stepfather—a friendly, gentle man—failed at a variety of occupations, forcing the little family to move frequently. By the time Jack was five years old, he had lived in nine different houses.

Jack London later wrote that he developed his lifelong reading habit when he was nine years old and first discovered [American author] Washington Irving's *The Alhambra* and other books about the long ago and far away. He discovered, to his delight, that at the Oakland [California] Public Library he could sign out all the books he wanted—and he wanted them all.

On the waterfront young Jack discovered other delights. He taught himself how to sail and spent many exciting hours on the San Francisco Bay. For a time, he was an "oyster pirate," robbing the commercial oyster beds by night and selling his illegal catch by day. Later, he joined the Fish Patrol to round up and drive out of business other pirates with whom he had once competed. These experiences London brought to life in a number of tales collected in two books, *The Cruise of the Dazzler* (1902) and *Tales of the Fish Patrol* (1905).

At the age of seventeen he sailed to the Sea of Japan aboard the *Sophia Sutherland*, a seal-hunting vessel, and when he returned home, his mother urged him to enter a writing competition sponsored by the *San Francisco Examiner*. He submitted "Typhoon Off the Coast of Japan," and this, his first published story, won the first prize: twenty-five dollars. Later, these experiences would help London write one of his best-known novels, *The Sea-Wolf* (1904), much of which takes place aboard a seal-hunter named *The Ghost*, whose captain is the brutal Wolf Larsen.

Student and Writer

When London returned to Oakland from his tramping trip, he enrolled in Oakland High School. Although he stayed only one year, he published a number of stories in the school's literary magazine, *The Aegis*. In the spring of 1896, bored and impatient with high school, he holed up in his tiny room and prepared for the college entrance examinations by studying nineteen hours a day. In a few months he learned—with the aid of some devoted friends—the entire high school curriculum, and in August he took the tests. And passed them.

In September, he enrolled in the University of California at nearby Berkeley, but because of financial difficulties he stayed only a single semester. He never returned to school.

Throughout the winter of 1896 London again holed up in his room, this time trying to make a living as a writer. He wrote a little bit of everything—stories, poems, plays, essays, and jokes. He mailed his efforts away to magazines, and one by one, every single item came back to him—rejected. He did not publish a word of his enormous daily output.

Finally, absolutely impoverished, he took a job in a laundry and became once again what he would later call a "work beast." He saw no end to the drudgery of physical labor. Later, London fictionalized many of these rough, frustrating experiences in his autobiographical novel *Martin Eden* (1909). Readers who wish to know about London's desperate struggle to become a writer have no better resource than this, his most personal book.

Gold! Gold! Gold!

On 14 July 1897, the steamship *Excelsior* arrived in San Francisco bearing a load of gold and miners with exciting tales to tell about an enormous gold strike in the Klondike River region of the Canadian Yukon. Tens of thousands of people quit their jobs, left their farms and shops and families, and headed northward.

Among the first to leave was Jack London. Racing against time because the Yukon River freezes in October, London and his companions landed at Dyea, Alaska, and packed their ton of supplies over the mountains to British Columbia, where they built two boats and began their five-hundred-mile float down the Yukon River to Dawson City, Yukon, center of the gold rush activity. But the north temporarily defeated them. About sixty miles short of Dawson, realizing that the river would soon be impassable, London and his companions decided to occupy some abandoned cabins. During the long winter London did a little prospecting, filed a claim, studied the theory of evolution in [British naturalist] Charles Darwin's *On the Origin of Species*, and greeted a wide variety of travelers—American Indians, Northwest Mounted Police, gold seekers, and government mail couriers.

On one visit to Dawson, London camped near the cabin of Louis and Marshall Bond, two brothers whose father, Judge Hiram G. Bond, owned a large ranch in Santa Clara, California. London was very impressed by one of the Bonds' dogs. It was a large animal, part Saint Bernard and part collie, named, oddly, Jack.

Stories into Gold

When he returned to California, London visited the Bonds, and he was so taken with their place that two years later, while writing what many consider his masterpiece, *The Call of the Wild* (1903), he placed the Bonds' dog Jack (now named Buck) on the ranch of Judge Bond (now called Judge Miller). Thus began the great adventure of the southland dog that is stolen from the ranch and taken to the northland, where he eventually leaves civilization to run with a pack of wolves.

London himself found little gold, but his year in the Klondike provided a resource even more precious: experience. Fashioned into powerful stories and novels and articles by his enormous imagination, this experience soon propelled him into worldwide celebrity. Jack London's pen would produce far more gold than any miner's pick or shovel.

His first book, *The Son of the Wolf: Tales of the Far North* (1900), is a collection of his earliest Klondike stories. *A Daughter of the Snows* (1902), his first novel, is about a woman named Frona Welse who seeks her fortune in the Klondike. *The Scorn of Women* (1906), his first play, is a Klondike love story. And throughout his career London continued to revisit the region in his writing, the final effort being *Smoke Bellew* (1912), published a few years before he died.

In addition to those already mentioned, the best known of these northland tales are *White Fang* (1906), a novel, and "To Build a Fire" (1910), a short story. London wrote *White Fang* as a companion to the hugely successful *The Call of the Wild*. He wished, he said, to reverse his earlier story of the civilized dog that returns to the wild. So White Fang, the wolf dog from the Yukon, returns at the end of the novel to the same California valley from which Buck had been stolen in *The Call of the Wild*.

"To Build a Fire," the tale of a foolish, unnamed man who meets his death on a bitterly cold day, is probably London's most frequently published short story. London set the tale in a region he knew well (it was on Henderson Creek that he had filed his own gold claim), and in no other story did he so clearly portray the fatal consequences of ignoring nature's laws and humanity's accumulated wisdom.

London's northland tales range widely in subject: from portrayals of people and animals struggling to survive in a bleak world governed by the harsh natural laws that Darwin had described, to examinations of the effects of the gold rush upon the native peoples in the region, to explorations of timeless human concerns like love and loyalty, dignity and self-respect, good and evil, crime and punishment, betrayal and revenge.

Marriage . . . and Love . . . and Marriage

On 17 April 1900, on the heels of his first literary successes, Jack London married [Elizabeth] Bessie May Maddern, a friend who had helped him pass his college entrance examinations. His other friends were surprised, for he had never really expressed any romantic interest in Bessie. On 15 January 1901, his first daughter, Joan, was born; on 20 October 1902, a second daughter, Becky, arrived.

In July 1903, the same month *The Call of the Wild* was published, London shocked his friends by leaving his wife and pursuing in public a relationship with another woman, Charmian Kittredge. On 17 November 1905, his divorce was finalized, and two days later he married Charmian. His daughters remained with their mother, and London was never again very close to either one of them.

Jack and Charmian were happy together, although they had no children and twice they suffered the heartbreak of miscarriage. Like her famous husband, Charmian loved the rugged outdoor life, and they spent many hours together swimming, sailing, horseback riding—and even boxing. Together they traveled to distant parts of the world, and Charmian helped Jack by typing his work (he wrote everything longhand) and by organizing and preserving his correspondence and manuscripts. Before he married Charmian, he had routinely discarded all his manuscripts once they were published.

The *Snark*

In 1905 London decided to build his own yacht and sail it with Charmian around the world on a seven-year cruise. They called the vessel the *Snark*, after a poem by [British writer] Lewis Carroll. London had by this time developed the habits of writing that he maintained throughout his career: He rose early each morning and wrote between 1,000 and 1,500 words. In the afternoon Charmian typed his morning's output, and

American author Jack London with his second wife, Charmian Kittredge, seated on a porch, 1914. © Everett Collection Historical/Alamy.

in the evening—and late into the night—he read books and magazines and edited what Charmian had typed for him. He continued this routine even while at sea; he performed it the day before he died.

On 22 April 1907, the *Snark*—after many delays and troubles—set sail for Hawaii and for what the Londons hoped would be seven years of continual adventure. When they arrived in Hawaii on 20 May, they learned from newspapers that they had been declared dead—all hands lost at sea!

After a rest in Hawaii—a spot they loved so well that they returned for an extended visit from 1915 to 1916—they sailed on, visiting Tahiti, Samoa, the Solomon Islands, and Australia. But by December both Jack and Charmian were so weakened by various ailments that they were forced to end their voyage, sell the *Snark*, and return to California.

London's travels in the South Seas figure in many of his stories, including his nonfiction account of his voyage, *The Cruise of the Snark* (1911). In 1915, Charmian also published a book about their journeys called *The Log of the Snark*. The principal stories appear in *South Sea Tales* (1911), *The House of Pride and Other Tales of Hawaii* (1912), *A Son of the Sun* (1912), and *The Red One* (1918).

A Wolf

In 1905 the Londons began buying ranch land in the Valley of the Moon region near Glen Ellen, California, about forty miles north of San Francisco. Jack had become greatly interested in agriculture and wanted to make his ranch a self-supporting community.

Although there was an old ranch house already on the property, the Londons planned to build a large stone home to be called Wolf House. On 22 August 1913, just as they were preparing to move in, a fire destroyed the building. For many years the origin of the fire was a mystery. But forensic scientists have recently determined that workers applying a finish to a fireplace mantel forgot to take with them their rags soaked in linseed oil. These rags ignited by spontaneous combustion. Wolf House had been insured for only a fraction of its original cost, and London did not have the money to rebuild. Today, the Jack London State Historic Park comprises much of the original ranch, and the ruins of Wolf House can still be seen. London wrote a number of stories set in his beloved Glen Ellen, including *The Valley of the Moon* (1913), *The Scarlet Plague* (1912), and *The Little Lady of the Big House* (1916).

"A World So New, So Terrible, So Wonderful"

Even while he was suffering personal tragedy (Charmian's miscarriages), personal loss (the disruption of the *Snark* voyage, the fire at Wolf House), and poor health, London maintained his daily writing routine. In the final months of his life, he began reading the works of the [Swiss] psychologist C.G. [Carl] Jung, who wrote about the unconscious mind and the power of myth. London told his wife that Jung's ideas were leading him to a "new" and "terrible" and "wonderful" world. He set to work using Jung's ideas in "The Red One" and "The Water Baby," two of his last stories.

But Jack London would not live long enough to explore this new psychological world. In November 1916, he was suffering from a variety of illnesses, some acquired on the *Snark* voyage. On 22 November he could not be awakened, and he died later that day on the porch of his ranch house. The attending physicians declared that the causes were uremia and kidney failure. Physicians today who have examined his symptoms and medical records have concluded that he probably suffered a stroke and heart failure as well.

Stories that Jack London died a suicide—stories that began in the late 1930s, probably instigated by a novel based on his life—have persisted even until today. They are false.

London's Love of the Wild Had a Dark Side

Charles Paul Freund

Charles Paul Freund is a senior editor for the magazine Reason, *where he writes about politics and culture. His writing has been published in the* Washington Post, New York Times, Esquire, *and numerous other newspapers and magazines.*

Freund lays out the case for the claim that Jack London was a racist who advocated for white superiority. London's belief in the absolute power of nature and his tales of heroic creatures fighting against the evils of civilization made him a favorite of the Communist left and the Fascist right. His books imply the presumed nobility and spiritual superiority of men in the wild. In looking to nature for morality, Freund claims, London was following a dangerous practice. For London, those opposed to the purity of nature are not just mistaken but immoral. Much of London's now ignored science fiction is filled with yellow-haired savages and primitive modern characters. He even wrote a story in which the white nations eliminated the Chinese by waging germ warfare. Freund suggests that all of this makes London a dubious hero for the modern age.

For a century, Jack London has been everyman's guide to the Yukon, and to a wilderness within. His best-known work, above all *The Call of the Wild* (1903), used the Canadian north to evoke a nature so primeval that it stripped away the superficial, the domesticated, and the merely social, and awakened the authentic man trapped inside. Recently, the modern Yukon sought to return London's tribute by honoring him. Now it has changed its mind.

The Skeleton in London's Closet

Why? Well, that howl piercing the northern night may sound like a wolf, but it is really the scream of environmentalism confronting one of the skeletons in its closet.

Here's what happened. The Yukon city of Whitehorse announced plans last year [1996] to rename one of its main streets Jack London Road. London was in the Yukon during its 1890s gold rush, leaving with only scurvy and his literary inspiration. Before Whitehorse could put up its new street signs, however, a local Indian tribe called the Kwanlin Dun objected. Some of London's personal letters, they charged, contained racist views. According to an account in the *Washington Post*, these "appeared to advocate white superiority." His defenders tried to save the day, arguing, in the *Post*'s words, that London "was relatively progressive for his era." But an embarrassed Whitehorse decided to drop London.

Actually, both of these characterizations—that London "appeared to advocate" racism, and that he was "relatively progressive"—are not only true, they are real understatements.

The nexus of these apparently inconsistent views is London's frequent subject: his idea of man's place in nature. Nor is London alone at the crossroads of politics, race, and nature. He is joined there by a number of other writers, most spectacularly by [Norwegian] Knut Hamsun, the Nobel Prize–winning novelist of the soil who was a favorite of both [Communist] Bolsheviks and [Fascist] Hitlerites, as well as by some of the nature activists of America's Progressive Era [1890s–1920s].

The Complex Politics of Nature

No literature has had so complex a political history in our century as that which addresses man amid nature, because no literature reveals so forcefully the riffs of industrialism at their hidden foundations. London's work is an instructive case in point. We may think of him as the author of *White Fang* and

American author Jack London is best known for his books The Call of the Wild *and* White Fang. © Pictorial Press Ltd./Alamy.

The Sea-Wolf, [German philosopher Friedrich] Nietzsche fit for boys (and with women now running with the wolves, for girls, too). But the Whitehorse incident caps a century of political turmoil around London; indeed, it is in some ways an inevitable climax to his literary adventure.

He actually invited much of this turmoil. Far from being just "relatively progressive," he was an admirer of [Karl Marx's] *The Communist Manifesto*: the original aw-shucks revolutionary in flannel. [American Communist] John Reed, still the poster boy of left-wing romantics, is a variation on the persona London pioneered. Even the now notorious valediction, "Yours for the Revolution," was first popularized by London. He was a marcher, a speech maker, and a propagandist for the overthrow of capitalism, and claimed his work had brought that event at least "ten minutes closer."

He also created a body of revolutionary fiction. The best known of these works is *The Iron Heel* (1908), described by H. Bruce Franklin (the noted science fiction authority and anthologizer of [Russian leader Joseph] Stalin) as "the epic struggle of the enslaved proletariat" against a predicted "20th-century Fascist oligarchy." London's now obscure socialistic stories are a fascinating combination of revolution and pulp luridness. "A Curious Fragment," for example, is built around the discovery of a 28th-century worker-slave's severed arm, still clutching a proletarian petition.

All this was very pleasing to, among others, [Russian leader Vladimir] Lenin, who regarded London as more useful culturally than such less thrilling writers as the constructivist poets, and who helped establish him as one of the few Americans to be a staple of popular Soviet reading.

But he was a lot less pleasing to his fellow American leftists. For one thing, there is some question about London's Marxist sincerity. Unlike [American novelist] Upton Sinclair, who squandered his wealth in utopian schemes, London spent his money on himself. He was also a critic of American socialists, resigning from the party in 1916 because it lacked "fire and fight." He thought World War I was a great opportunity, "a Pentecostal [baptismal] cleansing that can only result in good for humankind."

Nature-Racism

In the end, London's revolutionary hopes were really about undermining trade and technology. These alienated man from nature, turned him effete, and prevented him from realizing his destiny. That destiny was racial: A return to nature would free the blond Nordic beast. Critic Franklin notes that this theme runs through much of London's now ignored science fiction, from "The Strength of the Strong" to "When the World Was Young," which are filled with yellow-haired savages and atavistic [primitive] modern characters.

This sort of thing was to catch Germany's eye. German scholar Peter S. Fisher has noted the influence of London's fantasies on some of Weimar Germany's pulp racists, specifically his *The Scarlet Plague* (1912), which was read as "an accurate prophecy of the white race's demise." (It is noteworthy as well that *The Sea-Wolf*, which Soviets regarded as a tale of class injustice, was popular in Germany as a fable of the Will to Power.) The Nazis' preferred writer was the far more talented Knut Hamsun, a Norwegian who supported National Socialism [Nazism] because he believed trade and technology to be dehumanizing, and embraced its blood-and-soil nature mysticism.

But one needn't go overseas to connect London to nature-racism; it was rampant here. Americans in the 1890s were confronting the end of their frontier, and were pondering its meaning. One voice raised was that of [environmentalist] John Muir, who thought the wilderness was beautiful, and that it should not all be laid waste; most modern environmentalists will prefer to trace themselves to his aesthetic views.

But that's not where the populist action was. [President] Teddy Roosevelt, for example, supported wilderness preservation because he believed that men needed a place they could hunt; without such essentially manly activity Americans would become soft, decadent, deracinated. Historian Roderick Nash has traced the veritable cult of "savageness" that arose, celebrating the presumed nobility—and spiritual superiority—of men in the wild. A popular literature sprang up around such ideas, though only two of its practitioners still have readers: London and [American author and creator of *Tarzan*] Edgar Rice Burroughs.

Among those calling early for saving the redwoods and establishing wilderness preserves were such men as Madison Grant, the country's leading racial theoretician and a friend of TR's [Roosevelt's]. Author of the notorious book *The Passing of the Great Race*, Grant believed Nordics were being overwhelmed by inferior, merchant "races." Nordics couldn't compete with them because they, Nordics, were simply too magnificent for such mean competition. For Grant, the purpose of a saved wilderness was as a racial and spiritual redoubt [a fort]. . . .

The Danger of Absolutist Thinking

Nature, whether in Jack London's Klondike, Germany's Black Forest, or Russia's steppes, can be a source of beauty and renewal. Reasonable persons can take part in quotidian environmentalism, which is about recycling, pollution, and spotted owls, and not about racism or revolution. Why, then, have so many attuned themselves to murmuring pines and hemlocks, only to hear lessons in race hatred and bloodletting?

The answer lies in finding not merely beauty in nature, but absolutes. What nature-utopians of the left and right share is the belief that, whether in the peaceful rhythms of its seasons, in the unspoiled ruggedness of its landscapes, or in the tooth-and-claw struggle for survival, nature is a source both of wisdom and morality. From aesthetic to absolute is a short bridge to cross—some would argue it is an inevitable one—and even so moderate a figure as Muir went over it, ultimately preaching that the forests were God's true and sacrosanct cathedral. . . .

But spiritual cathedral or racial redoubt, once one perceives nature as good in the absolute, the alternatives to its purity become not just mistaken, but immoral. Thus commerce and machinery are not just distractions; because they alienate us from nature, they are evil, as are their users, defenders, and beneficiaries.

Concepts of evil derived from the absolutist contemplation of nature flourished earlier in this century; scholar Anna Bramwell traces that remarkable history in *Ecology in the 20th Century* (1989). Environmentalism's rise has, by the logic of ideas, buoyed many such notions back into view: from the mystical antipathy to machinery to goddess worship; from Unabomber terrorism [of Ted Kaczynski] to the Gaia thesis [that organisms evolve with their environment] of a sentient Earth. Left-wing activist and journalist Michael Novick has written of the xenophobes who have attached themselves to environmentalism under the guise of population control, and reports a number of small-time revivals of racist blood-and-soil movements in Europe. American racist Tom Metzger has attempted to combine the Aryan movement here with ecologism; the Fascist gathering in the Northwest is an attempt to realize Nordland, their racist nature Utopia.

That German nature-mysticism got wrapped up in National Socialism does not mean that such ideas have an inevitable trajectory. But as it happens, London himself imaginatively preceded the Nazis along their racist path all the way to genocide. In his awful story "The Unparalleled Invasion," the world's white nations unite to wage germ warfare against the Chinese, killing them all, and inaugurating a golden age.

Whitehorse cancelled its Jack London Road. But in a sense there is one anyway, and it is worth pondering where it leads, and where, at any given time, we might be along it.

Jack London Was Not a Racist

Dan Davidson and the Klondike Sun Staff

Dan Davidson writes for the Klondike Sun, *which is located in Dawson City, Yukon, the setting of some of London's most famous tales.*

In the following viewpoint from the Klondike Sun, *Dan Davidson answers the charges that Jack London was a racist. Davidson cites Professor Susan Nuernberg, a London expert, who claims that although many of London's characters display racist attitudes, this thinking should not be confused with London's own views on race. In fact, Nuernberg says, London's stories consistently show an enlightened attitude toward race, as opposed to the more common racist attitudes displayed by many writers of London's time. What really got London into trouble with his contemporaries was his creation of fiercely independent female characters and his negative attitude toward capitalism— and not any perceived racism.*

When some folks in Whitehorse wanted to rename Two Mile Hill [Road] last year [in 1996], they thought that Jack London Blvd. would make a good replacement. At the same time the South Access Road was slated to be transformed into Robert Service Way [after the Scottish Canadian poet].

Racist or Not?

Citizens rose in arms to battle against the first proposed change, probably because the existing name suited the hill to a tee. In the end advocates of Jack London Blvd. were thwarted by the ultimate weapon of these politically correct times when a cluster of protesters decided to trump their proposals by playing the race card.

Jack London, said some people, was a racist. His works reflected a view of the world unsuitable for commemoration, a view that would be insulting to our First Nations citizens.

Not so, says London scholar Professor Susan Nuernberg of the University of Wisconsin-Oshkosh, one of the keynote speakers at last weekend's Jack London Festival. Her lecture, entitled "The Idea of Race in Jack London's Early Yukon Stories," ranged even further than its title would indicate, but it certainly tackled the race issue head-on and appeared to give it a thrashing.

There's no denying, says Nuernberg, that London would probably have placed the white race ahead of others on his individual scale of values. That would have been normal for a liberally educated young man of his time, and was certainly normal for the culture from which he sprang. His training, education and commercial awareness of his reading audience would all have pointed him in this direction.

Mistaken Attribution

What's amazing then, is that he didn't take that path, choosing instead to write against the grain of this notion. While it is certainly possible to pick racist-sounding statements out of London's works, Nuernberg says that most of them come from the mouths of his characters and are there for a purpose.

"While examples like these abound in his fiction, the assumption that London's own views coincide with those mouthed by his characters is completely mistaken," [she said.]

Assuming that London necessarily shared those sentiments is a mistake that many people make about authors and their stories. It's a bit like deciding that the English poet John Milton was a satanist after reading some of the dialogue he gives to the devil in his epic poem *Paradise Lost*.

What happened instead was that London captured in print the views and ideas of the people about whom he was writing.

His popularity stemmed in part from his ability to do this. People recognized themselves in his writing.

London vs. Common Nineteenth-Century Thought

Nuernberg spent part of her lecture dissecting London's first novel, *A Daughter of the Snows* [published in 1902], which followed his first story collection, *The Son of the Wolf.* This novel is not widely known and was not a great success, but it does contain some fairly clear examples of what Nuernberg feels were London's actual opinions on the subject of race.

Encapsulated, the story features a young woman, Frona Welse, of very definitely racist opinions who goes north and falls in with two young men. One of them, Gregory St. Vincent, seems to be the very embodiment of the Teutonic ideal, while the other, Vance Corliss, is a more thoughtful fellow. The story is a romance and deals with how this triad works itself out. In the end the Teutonic chap turns out to be a skunk, the girl changes many of her opinions about race theory and settles on the other fellow, who was much more enlightened and felt Frona's ideas "were dangerous and poorly thought out."

She compared London's work to that of other well-known writers of his day, particularly that of Theodore Roosevelt, who eventually became a president of the United States. Roosevelt's bombastic style was filled with racial stereotypes and negative commentary about Indians, blacks and Spaniards.

This tendency goes right back to the roots of the American pedagogical system, beginning with Thomas Jefferson, and carries on until after the Second World War. Nuernberg noted that there was an American tendency to idealize the Teutonic or Aryan race until after the defeat of the Nazis, when the fullest implications of this way of thinking finally became clear.

Enlightened Views on Race

For the most part, she said, Jack London used Native American ("First Nations" in Canada) characters as foils for his white protagonists. His most famous single short story, "To Build a Fire," shows the stupidity of a newly arrived, "civilized" Cheechako as compared with everyone else he meets in the story. The man freezes to death because he doesn't take the advice he has been given.

In his novel about poverty in Europe, *The People of the Abyss*, Nuernberg says London pronounced that "only in civilization do people starve in the midst of plenty" and compared capitalist society unfavorably with that of the natives he had met living along the Yukon River.

Said Nuernberg, "London's Native American characters are used as an allegory to point up the shortcomings of civilization."

In *A Daughter of the Snows*, St. Vincent, the cad, is eventually contrasted unfavorably with an aboriginal character in the story, "who never knew Western civilization, but still can exhibit to them a sense of honour and courage," [Nuernberg said.]

Compared with other writers of his day and time, Nuernberg feels that Jack London's views on race were "enlightened." What got him into more trouble at the time he wrote was his habit of creating fiercely independent female characters whose impact on his stories was quite at variance with the established norms of his day. That, and the social critique of capitalism inherent in a lot of his work, was what stirred people against him in North America, while at the same time gaining him a loyal following in Europe.

London's Yukon Trip Changed His Life

James L. Haley

James L. Haley has written an award-winning biography of Sam Houston as well as The Buffalo War: The History of the Red River Indian Uprising of 1874 *and* Passionate Nation: The Epic History of Texas. *He is also the author of three novels.*

In this biographical viewpoint, Haley writes that Jack London was the illegitimate son of a rebellious mother and an astrologer father who left her before his birth. From his earliest years, London struggled to overcome his uncertain beginnings. He worked at numerous menial jobs and traveled across the country. He was largely self-educated, only enrolling in high school at an advanced age, then spending a few months in college. His mother, recognizing his innate talent, urged him to enter a writing contest, which he won. But his subsequent attempts at publishing were met with rejection. When the Yukon gold rush commenced in 1897, London left to seek his fortune. Instead of finding gold, Haley says, London found his calling. In an epiphany that came to him while enduring the harsh Yukon winter, London realized that he would become a writer.

On July 14, 1897, the steamship *Excelsior* docked in San Francisco, California. It brought with it the first news that gold had been discovered in the Klondike region of the Canadian Yukon. Unremarkable men who once had only modest means now swaggered down the gangplank with gold dust and nuggets enough to set themselves up in business and

James L. Haley, *Wolf: The Lives of Jack London.* New York: Basic Books, 2010, pp. 1–5. Copyright © 2005 by Perseus Book Group. All rights reserved. Reproduced by permission.

live—some comfortably, a few fabulously. The news rocked the country to its foundations, not least because it gave hope to America's teeming ranks of the poor.

The United States was still wallowing in the malaise of the Panic of 1893 and its subsequent depression. The economic excesses of what [American writer] Mark Twain had called the Gilded Age, the high-water mark of unrestrained capitalism and gaudy wealth for the tiny class of industrialist robber barons, now cruelly tormented the lower class. Jobs were scarce and miserably paid; the standard wage for backbreaking labor was ten cents an hour. Shirkers and troublemakers, and especially anyone who even looked like he might be a unionizer or a socialist, were fired in a heartbeat and replaced from the long line of the unemployed who were desperate to have that dime an hour.

Typical of them—in fact, archetypical of them—was a disaffected young intellectual of twenty-one who drifted about the dockside bars of Oakland, California. He was the illegitimate son of an unbalanced, free-loving spiritualist mother, who had been steadied somewhat by marriage to a kindly but partially disabled Civil War veteran. The boy was sensitive and unusually gifted, and he came to adore books, but in his existence there was little time to read.

A Series of Chores

From his earliest memory, life had been little more than a series of chores. As soon as he left primary school he had been set to work in a cannery, stuffing pickles into jars for the ubiquitous ten cents an hour. At fifteen he realized he could make vastly more money as a thief. He borrowed the funds to buy a small sloop, taught himself to sail, and became an oyster pirate, raiding San Francisco Bay's guarded tidal farms that were the monopoly of the Southern Pacific Railroad. He bought rounds of drinks for the waterfront toughs who became his friends, hiding from them his love of books and learning. Wary of prison or the violent death that other pirates met, he soon switched sides and made a small living for a while as a deputy for the California Fish Patrol.

Still poor, seventeen, and suffocating, he signed aboard a sealing schooner hoping that his share of the profits would rescue his family from their poverty. He was at sea for seven months, pulling his boat, slaughtering seals, and fending off the bullying and indecent advances of older sailors. Alone on his watch he had steered the ship through a roaring typhoon and returned home a man. But the little money he made was soon gone.

The economy had crashed during his absence, and he was lucky to find a job loading bobbins in a jute mill—for ten cents an hour. Knowing his love of books and gift of expression, his mother urged him to enter a literary contest sponsored by a local newspaper. Sacrificing precious hours of sleep, he wrote of the typhoon off the coast of Japan, and won the first prize of $25—a month's wages. It set him on a flurry of writing other articles, but no one would buy them.

He had read Horatio Alger stories as a boy, and still needed to believe that he could rise as a result of his honest labor. He took a job shoveling coal in the powerhouse of an electric railway company. The manager promised that he could advance in the business if he started at the bottom. The pay was $30 a month: ten hours a day, seven days a week—only they habitually gave him at least twelve hours' worth of coal to shovel. His actual pay was even less than a dime an hour. His whole body would seize up with cramps, and he sprained his wrists, forcing him to wear heavy leather splints to do the job. Advancement never came, and another employee eventually confessed that in shoveling coal he was the replacement of two men, who had been paid forty dollars a month—each.

He quit in a rage and became a hobo, riding the rails and experiencing the penniless subculture of vagrancy. To his surprise he met brilliantly read men among the tramps, men who introduced him to the egalitarian doctrines of socialism and gave him a cause to live for. Their disdain for capitalism and its minions who enforced order and conformity became brutally vivid in Buffalo, New York, where he was unjustly imprisoned for a month after being denied access to a lawyer.

Trouble with Education

He worked his way back home and returned to high school. He was years older than the other students. Some of his classmates mocked him for earning his keep as the school janitor, but others were mesmerized by the stories he wrote of his wide-roaming life, no fewer than eight of which were published in the school's literary journal. Looking ahead to college, he entered a prep school but was soon dismissed. The headmaster determined that he could not afford to have their wealthy students outshone by this working-class ruffian.

Stung but defiant, he studied on his own, and passed the three-day entrance exam to the University of California at Berkeley. He borrowed the tuition from a kindly barkeeper, but family poverty forced him to withdraw after a single semester. The institution was not sorry to see him go, for his effectiveness as an editorialist and street-corner socialist was raising consternation among students and faculty alike. He returned to his labors, for ten cents an hour, ironing shirts in the steam laundry—exquisite irony—of a prep school.

In Search of Gold

When the *Excelsior* docked with news of gold in the Yukon, the young malcontent knew he had to go. That there would be adventure was certain. There was also the possibility of wealth, perhaps great wealth. He approached his stepsister to lend him the money for a "grubstake." He was uncertain whether she would support him, until he discovered that her much older husband had also determined to go seek a fortune.

Only eleven days after the *Excelsior* had tied up, the pair boarded a coastal steamer dangerously overloaded with hundreds of other hopeful Klondikers, and headed north. They changed ships in Seattle and engaged an Indian canoe in Juneau to paddle them the last hundred miles to the prospectors' beachhead at Dyea.

He was greeted with chaos. Three thousand would-be prospectors, nearly all of them *Cheechakoes*, the derisive local term for a tenderfoot, were all trying to get themselves organized to hike into the gold fields. It was nearly a three-week haul just to reach the first large resting camp, after which the elevation increased more and more steeply. London had brought a half ton of supplies, all of which he had to carry in on his back, lugging seventy-five to one hundred pounds in each one-mile stage before trekking back for another load.

Many of his ill-prepared competitors had stupidly brought horses to do their hauling. This was a country with no forage. Overloaded and whipped, the horses soon dropped dead or fell into ravines. All his life he had adored horses, and now he saw to his horror how Dead Horse Gulch got its name.

The last obstacle was the worst. Chilkoot Pass presented him with a trek of three-quarters of a mile, upward at a 45-degree angle, after which the Canadian authorities at the border were satisfied that he could maintain himself and motioned him on. From there, he and his partners reached Lindeman Lake, the headwaters of the Yukon, where they built boats to float down to the gold region.

"Float," he discovered, did not begin to describe the terrors that followed. The lakes were connected by rivers fraught with gargantuan rapids. They saw others' boats dashed on rocks, or swallowed by gaping whirlpools. Men drowned before their eyes. Miraculously they made it through to Bennett Lake and Tagish Lake, and his sailing experience on San Francisco Bay got them through to Marsh Lake, which poured out into the gruesome rapids of 50-Mile River. As other outfits

Jack London's historic house in Dawson City, Yukon, Canada. He lived in this log house with a sod-and-grass roof while in the Yukon prospecting gold. © WLB Photogarphy/ Alamy.

came to grief, and death, on chutes called the Ridge and the Horse's Mane, he got them through to Lake Laberge, and there winter overtook them.

Twice they were defeated by icy headwinds while trying to cross the lake before it froze. The third time they sailed by night, exiting the lake into 30-Mile River just in time to see the sheet of ice form behind them. Outfits less hardy would have to spend the winter where they were.

Almost at their destination, only eighty miles from the freezing boomtown of Dawson, they were met by discouraged would-be prospectors on their way back. The good claims had already been staked, they said, and there was barely enough food in town to get through the winter—a bad omen for them and the thousands of others who had come north to get rich. He and his partners appropriated an abandoned line shack and set up housekeeping, having decided they might as well hunker down for the advancing Arctic winter where they were, and conditions were deteriorating steadily.

A Personal Epiphany

Some days after, he set off alone up a nearby creek to do some exploratory panning, sheltering himself in a log dugout. The gold he found amounted to no more than a fingertip of flakes. Already he was showing the early signs of "Klondike Plague": scurvy. His gums bled, and his skin was slack and pallid. A passing doctor told him he would die without medical care. He could not go back the way he came; if he lived until the ice broke he would somehow have to sail down the entire length of the Yukon to civilization.

In this frozen crucible he reached a personal epiphany. He would never advance in life as a laborer. When he could no longer shovel coal he would be tossed aside like any other used-up, disabled worker. He had just turned twenty-two; if he lived through this winter, he vowed to himself, he would become a writer. If people were ignorant, he would educate them. If society was unjust, he would preach justice. He had shown a talent for writing; if he made it back home, he would train himself to write professionally, no matter what it took.

Cold, sick, lonely and miserable, the young man whose penmanship had never developed beyond what he could manage in grammar school scrawled some highly prophetic graffiti onto the log next to his bunk:

Jack London Miner Author Jan 27, 1898

Wildness in
The Call of the Wild

Jack London's Enduring Appeal

Eric Miles Williamson

Eric Miles Williamson has taught at the University of Texas-Pan American and at the University of Central Missouri. He is the author of Oakland, Jack London, and Me, *as well as several novels.*

Williamson observes in the following viewpoint that although Jack London was once the most popular author in the world, he has long since fallen out of favor with the literary establishment. Contemporary critics desire literature that is difficult to read and rewards those who want to translate the author's esoteric language into understandable concepts. London was a straightforward author whose work is powerful, but not particularly cryptic. Nevertheless, London has come back into prominence as a "literary whipping boy," Williamson maintains, for those who want to find fault with his attitudes toward race, politics, and gender. Williamson defends London, however, as a writer who challenges readers to face their own isolation and alienation. In his works, London strips away the veneer of civilization and writes powerfully about how characters react when confronting a vast, brutal, and indifferent world.

More than a hundred years ago, in 1898, Jack London sold his first short story to the San Francisco–based magazine, *Overland Monthly*, for five dollars. A year later, he landed "Odyssey of the North" with *Atlantic Monthly*, and from there he went on to become the first American author to become a millionaire on his writing, to become America's

Eric Miles Williamson, "Jack London's Enduring Appeal," *Virginia Quarterly Review*, vol. 75, no. 4, Autumn 1999, pp. 787–92. Copyright © 1999 by The University of Virginia. All rights reserved. Reproduced by permission.

most famous author, to become a celebrity akin to a movie star of today. London's works have been translated into more than 60 languages, and he remains the best-selling American author in the world.

London's general treatment by the academic community, however, has been less than respectful. The English professorate [professors] in America has only recently deigned to acknowledge his works as something worthy of study.

Contemporary critics tend to prefer works that they can decode, performing explicatory wizardry for students who had mistakenly believed that they could read. [American experimental author] Gertrude Stein, [Irish novelist] James Joyce, and [American poet] T. S. Eliot generate ten articles per every article on [American novelist] John Steinbeck, [American poet] Robert Frost, and [American novelist] Willa Cather, and the reason is pretty simple: the former triumvirate is linguistically more difficult than the latter trio. [American experimental novelist] Thomas Pynchon's tome *Gravity's Rainbow* has become an industry, and though the linguistic fireworks of the book are impressive indeed, who can *read* the thing? [American novelist William] Gaddis' *JR* is brilliant, certainly, but in the final analysis it just might be more work to read than is worth the while. These books, however, dwarf the Nobel Prize efforts of [popular American novelists] Sinclair Lewis, of Steinbeck, of Pearl S. Buck, and the efforts of Jack London. For my money, though, George's dilemma at the end of [Steinbeck's novel] *Of Mice and Men* is far more poignant than Eliot's chant, "This is the way the world ends." The simplicity of Sinclair Lewis, of Cather, of London, however, doesn't provide contemporary academic critics, who increasingly see themselves in the position of translators to English from the English, with much to do.

Until recently, London has been viewed as a curiosity, as a writer of popular fiction in the adventure genre who happened a couple of times to mysteriously knock out a good story, a story which nearly, but not quite, measured up to American academic aesthetic standards. The "good" stories are the ones which create the need for translation, for solving the unsolvable moral dilemmas presented. "An Odyssey of the North," "To Build a Fire," *The Call of the Wild*, and *White Fang* have generated periodic condescending interest or crude careerist interest—professors writing about his work because it was an "open field" and generated an easy publication—but college students are more likely to be assigned secondhand speeches by [Suquamish Native American] Chief Seattle and anonymous African tribal chants than they are the works of Jack London.

There are readily several identifiable reasons why London has been kept off the reading lists. The main reason, of course, that London has been neglected is because his dog stories, *The Call of the Wild* and *White Fang*, are so good, so *simple*: the profs, when presenting London's best work, simply have nothing to decode. More invidious reasons for not assigning the works begin with the fact that London's socialism has not been in vogue, and professors reared in the 50s and tenured in the 60s when there were more professorships available than PhDs to fill them have shunned London like they have [American novelist John] Dos Passos, Steinbeck, and Sinclair Lewis for obvious reasons—capitalism worked pretty damned well for them, after all. As well as being a Commie, London was an outspoken racist, and, of course, this will not do: Evolutionist theories are applied to everything *except* modern mankind, as we live in enlightened times during which *every* human being is absolutely *equal* with the exception of sports stars. London's essay, "The Yellow Peril," an essay about the Japanese and the threat London saw them as posing to the West, is often cited as evidence of his racism—never mind the fact that he was *right* to fear the Japanese, who, a generation later, invaded China, bombed Pearl Harbor, enslaved the Koreans, and proved to be some of the most joyous defilers of humanity recent history has witnessed. Also working against London in recent times is his machismo: He is a *man*—a man who drank and beat seals to death with a club and labored in factories and felt there was a difference between men and women: and this has not served him well. Witness the treatment [American novelist Ernest] Hemingway has received in recent years: Scores of articles have been written about what a disgusting macho cad Hemingway was, many of the critics accusing Hemingway of being a latent homosexual. Being a man, in the traditional sense of the word, has worked against London, and, like Hemingway, he has begun to be looked upon with the smirk of Gender and Queer Theorists [those who study gay literature]. The list goes on: He is white, male, racist, macho, sexist, anti-intellectual, Fascist, Communist, mercenary, aesthetically simplistic, poorly educated, a drunkard, a showboat, a hypocrite. Those who would promote a literary canon based on aesthetic principles scoff at London's supposedly stone-mitted style and crude autodidacticism [self-learning], and those who would base entry into the canon on political considerations deplore London for his failure to espouse the tenets of today's supra-democratic aesthetic liberalism. No matter what your cause, you won't have to look hard to find something to hate about Jack London. London is everything contemporary academics despise.

Which is why, in the past decade, he has come back into vogue.

Not as a literary figure, but as a literary whipping boy.

No easier target has ever taken up the pen in this country, and in the climate of hatred (hatred for the canon, hatred for white males, hatred for those who aren't white males, hatred for those who would reconfigure the canon, hatred for aesthetics and for anti-aesthetics, and so forth) which characterizes the universally fractured English departments around the country, London is a writer who can be trotted out, shoved to his knees, and flogged without let and without objection. For those who would seek an icon of the white male oppressor, they need look no further than London: He's a crowd pleaser for Marxists [after German economist Karl Marx], feminists, multiculturalists, African Americanists, post colonialists [those who study countries once under imperialist rule] and the practitioners of the rest of the isms which pluralize literary think tanks today. London's great works are currently being scrutinized for hints of racism, sexism, elitism, and so forth, and when the offense is detected, he is denounced. And on the occasions when his works don't supply the necessary information for dismantling his reputation, the critics turn to his biography.

In Alex Kershaw's *Jack London: A Life*, Kershaw remains neutral on London's politics, philosophies, and offenses. Instead of concentrating on the mental life of an author who spent the most part of his waking hours reading and writing (London produced nearly 50 books in less than 20 years of writing), Kershaw gives us a biography which reflects the sordid tastes of our times, concentrating on London's drinking, his sex life, his various "adventures" (after nearly a century of anticipation, for instance, we finally discover what kind of bloomers London's second wife, Charmian, wore on their wedding night)—the aspects of London's life which make for a book that reads like a novelization of a movie. In Kershaw's biography, London would seem to knock off volumes of fiction and essays as if he were tossing back shots of whiskey. As London is presented in this book, it would seem he spent very little time writing at all, very little time alone in his study.

But London spent plenty of time alone and considering the nature of isolation. Part of the perennial appeal of London is that he is able to show us what we are when we are in solitude, for it is only in solitude that we discover that thing which some call God. In his story "The White Silence," London writes,

Author Jack London writing in the outdoors. © Bettmann/Corbis/AP Images.

Nature has many tricks wherewith she convinces man of his finity—the ceaseless flow of the tides, the fury of the storm, the shock of the earthquake, the long roll of heaven's artillery—but the most tremendous, the most stupefying of all, is the passive phase of the White Silence. All movement ceases, the sky clears, the heavens are as brass; the slightest whisper seems sacrilege, and man becomes timid, affrighted at the sound of his own voice. Sole speck of life journeying across the ghostly wastes of a dead world, he trembles at his audacity, realizes that his is a maggot's life, nothing more. Strange thoughts arise unsummoned, and the mystery of all things strives for utterance. And the fear of death, of God, of the universe, comes over him—the hope of the Resurrection and the Life, the yearning for immortality, the vain striving of the imprisoned essence—it is then, if ever, man walks alone with God.

In America today, the notion of solitude is a fading thing, and we grow ever more godless. As the communications era develops, we are increasingly unable to ever sense our solitary personalities. The work of [British novelist] Jane Austen and [American novelist] Henry James has tellingly come back into vogue, and their lesser works are being canvassed for film possibilities—we're in an era that would much rather know about how people interact socially than how people behave when they're in isolation. Americans don't much want to consider Man Alone. We define ourselves in terms of our relationship to society, and even infants are now required to have Social Security numbers. What we actually *are* becomes increasingly difficult to ascertain. London says that we're beasts. In his essay "The Somnambulists," he writes,

Chained in the circle of his own imaginings, man is only too keen to forget his origin and to shame that flesh of his that bleeds like all flesh and that is good to eat. Civilization (which is part of the circle of his imaginings) has spread a veneer over the surface of the soft-shelled animal known as man. It is a very thin veneer; but so wonderfully is man constituted that he squirms on his bit of achievement and believes he is garbed in armor-plate.

Yet man to-day is the same man that drank from his enemy's skull in the dark German forests, that sacked cities, and stole his women from neighboring clans like any howling aborigine. The flesh-and-blood body of man has not changed in the last several thousand years. Nor has his mind changed.

It's not that we have changed, but that we have managed to shield ourselves from ourselves, that we have figured out ways to avoid our inner selves, that we have constructed society in such a manner that we do not have to deal with the remote tinglings of our animality. When we are offended, we do not strike out with a fist—there are laws to prevent us from this animal behavior. No, instead we sue the offender and ruin his life, get him fired from his job, take all the money he has worked for, send him to the poorhouse. Our ability to shield ourselves from solitude has increased to such a point that by *law* in this country we cannot exist outside of society. We're that afraid.

We don't know who we are, and we generally don't want to know. We don't want to know what beasts we really are, and we don't want to know what we'd do if we were in a situation like that of the Donner Party [who resorted to cannibalism] snowed in for the winter on the roof of the Sierras.

Jack London wants us to know.

London, like [American novelist Mark] Twain and [American novelist James Fenimore] Cooper before him, removes his characters from the drawing rooms of Europe and sends them into nature—in London's case, to the wilderness of the northland—and the rules, away from the paradigms of formal society, are left for London to derive from nature and from his characters' own souls. London works toward his own metaphysical system, and in order to develop that system, he must get man alone and by himself in the vastness of a brutal and indifferent cosmos.

London's appeal is universal because try as we might to convince ourselves that we are otherwise, we are subject to the whims of nature and circumstance. We are creatures of the flesh, and the flesh is rotting. London plucks a universal string because he is concerned with the primordial condition of man's isolation, an isolation that is shared by all humanity whether in a metropolis or on a pot farm in Kentucky. Our alienation is eternal, and if we're not feeling alienated, it's probably because we're stoned on the comforts of this great land of gluttony.

On Primitivism in
The Call of the Wild

Richard Fusco

*Richard Fusco is a professor of English at Saint Joseph's Univer-
sity in Pennsylvania. He specializes in nineteenth-century literature and the short story. His books include* Maupassant and the
American Short Story: The Influence of Form at the Turn of
the Century.

*Fusco argues in the following viewpoint that critics who
claim Buck descends into complete primitivism at the end of* The
Call of the Wild *misinterpret London's story. Basing his argument on philosopher Jean-Jacques Rousseau's four stages of man's
development—from the primitive to a transitional state to a
family social unit stage and finally to modern civilization—
Fusco suggests that Buck, too, goes through these stages. Instead
of finding chaos and utter primitivism at the story's conclusion,
however, Buck settles into a family unit with his new companions, the wolves. This ideal family, Fusco claims, allows Buck's
instincts a freer bent, even as he does not completely surrender
to the wild.*

Jack London's *The Call of the Wild* traces one animal's
gradual reversion to its primordial instincts. During the
course of the novel the dog Buck experiences a gamut of life
styles from civilization to apparent primitiveness. If a reader
analyzes the story only superficially, he could erroneously con-
clude that London's protagonist does indeed surrender totally
to ancient urges, which the author identifies as "the call of the
wild." Buck's metamorphosis is not as complete as a cursory

Richard Fusco, "On Primitivism in *The Call of the Wild*," *American Literary Realism
1870–1910*, vol. 20, no. 3, Fall 1987, pp. 76–80. Copyright © 1987 by American Literary
Realism. All rights reserved. Reproduced by permission.

reading might lead one to believe, however. Buck still retains vestiges of social advancement in his eventual leadership of the wolf pack. In preparing for the wild, the dog undergoes a socialization process of three stages, each represented by Buck's dealings with a differing sort of family. His fourth and final, ideal family resembles the compromise between civilization and primitive man [Swiss-French philosopher Jean-Jacques] Rousseau described for the idealized political state. Thus, London's concept of a propitious universe is not nature operating in chaos, but instinct tempered somewhat by learning.

Curiously, this misinterpretation of *The Call of the Wild* resembles in form a misconception critics often harbor about Rousseau's ideal society. Arthur O. Lovejoy identifies this problem as "[t]he notion that Rousseau's *Discourse on Inequality* was essentially a glorification of the state of nature, and that its influence tended wholly or chiefly to promote 'primitivism,' is one of the most persistent of historical errors." Lovejoy describes Rousseau's four phases of man's development as (1) a primitive, animalistic stage, (2) a transitory stage, (3) a family-scale social unit stage, and (4) modern civilization. Rousseau did reject the artificiality of contemporary society, but he did not suggest that men revert to the first stage of their development. Lovejoy points out:

> Rousseau could not bring himself to accept either extreme as his ideal; the obvious way out, therefore, was to regard the mean between these extremes as the best state possible. In the third stage, men were less good-natured and less placid than in the state of nature, but also were less stupid and less unsocial; they were less intelligent and had less power over nature than civilized man, but were also less malicious and less unhappy. In thus regarding the state of savagery, which some have called the "state of nature," not as a kind of natural perfection, an absolute norm, but as a mixed condition, intermediate between two extremes equally undesirable, Rousseau once more differed profoundly from his primitivistic predecessors.

Swiss-French philosopher Jean-Jacques Rousseau believed there were four stages of man's development from primitive stage to full integration into society. © Bettmann/Corbis/AP Images.

Consequently, Rousseau saw small clans as the best of all possible political and social structures, permitting the healthiest compromise between reason and instinct.

Although no biographical evidence exists that Rousseau's writings directly influenced *The Call of the Wild*, London apparently employed a similar philosophic system in constructing his novel. *The Call of the Wild* does trace one character's eventual rejection of the artificialities of modern society in favor of a clan-type existence. Buck's associations with four families symbolize the phases of his regression to the wild. First, for four years Buck lived on Judge Miller's "sun-kissed Santa Clara Valley" ranch. London presents Buck as a fully integrated member of Miller's family and, hence, of civilization. Despite Buck's avoidance of "becoming a mere pampered house-dog," his life is carefree—especially when compared to the harsher fate that awaits him. His relations with other "family members"—both men and animals—arouse Buck's impulse to dominate those around him, but his power has no foundation. His chief flaw lies in his innocence: He knows nothing of mankind's treachery. Consequently, a gardener's helper easily steals and sells the dog because of the latter's naive trust of all men. Buck's early life in California contains another, more glaring superficiality, though—the absence of love:

> This [love] he had never experienced at Judge Miller's down in the sun-kissed Santa Clara Valley. With the Judge's sons, hunting and tramping, it had been a working partnership; with the Judge's grandsons, a sort of pompous guardianship; and with the Judge himself a stately and dignified friendship.

In sum, the civilization that Miller's ranch represents has underdeveloped Buck's potential—both emotional and otherwise.

On one hand, Buck's second family, the dog sled team, places the dog in a world apparently stripped of civilization's veneer. After weathering the shock of his transition to a bleak and brutal existence, Buck attempts to dominate his new world and does succeed in establishing his authority over the team. On the other hand, the order and purpose of his new family bear the artificial imprint of civilization, represented by the men who drive the sled. The team exists not for its own benefit but to transport men and mail. Consequently, the team must suffer the whims of its human masters. When a backlog of Yukon mail must be delivered, Buck's tired family must transport it. Later, three greenhorn miners buy the team and set out upon a foolhardy journey. The family must follow its owners through exhaustion and to death. Only providence and John Thornton save Buck. Although Buck's primordial instincts begin to awaken while with the team, he also learns much on a conscious level, particularly about the dynamics within family relationships. He uses this knowledge to assert authority not only over the dog team but also later over the wolf pack, his final family.

Buck's third family consists of John Thornton, his partners, and his dogs, which represent a further phase of Buck's advancement toward the wild. In many ways Buck's life with Thornton resembles his life with Miller. It differs, though, in that love rather than "stately and dignified friendship" bonds the dog and the miner. Thornton's family is still not ideal, however, because Buck remains subject to man's caprices. For example, to see how far Buck will go in obeying him, Thornton orders the dog to leap over a steep cliff. Only by tackling Buck does the miner prevent the dog from doing so. Later, Buck must pull a sled loaded with a thousand pounds of flour because a rival miner had maneuvered Thornton into a foolish bet. For the most part, though, the good-natured Thornton forbears asking Buck to do anything with a superficial motive behind it. In fact, except for two life-threatening events, the miner requires little of Buck's services. He allows the dog the freedom to roam the wilderness alone, during which time Buck perfects his survival skills. Through these solitary hunting trips Buck realizes that he can live without man. His only remaining link with civilization lies in his love for Thornton. Consequently, Thornton's death at the hands of the Yeehats releases the dog from all obligations.

Buck does not remain alone: He joins a fourth family—a wolf pack, signifying his rejection of the total primitiveness of an anarchic wilderness. Eventually, based upon the principles of love and survival he learned as a member of his three former families, he assumes the leadership of the pack. Under Buck's direction the pack exhibits behavioral characteristics beyond those governed by instinct. For example, in killing the Indians who murdered Thornton, Buck conquers his fear of man:

> He had killed man, the noblest game of all, and he had killed in the face of the law of club and fang. He sniffed the bodies curiously. They had died so easily. It was harder to kill a husky dog than them. They were no match at all, were it not for their arrows and spears and clubs. Thenceforward he would be unafraid of them except when they bore in their hands their arrows, spears, and clubs.

The dog brings this knowledge to his new family, and, in consequence, the pack becomes more prone to attack stray Yeehat hunters than ever before. The wolf pack becomes so fierce that the Indians ascribe supernatural traits to it. Every autumn during moose season hunters refuse to enter the "certain valley" where Buck, the "Ghost Dog," rules.

In sum, Buck's ideal family permits his instincts freer bent, but, as Rousseau recommends, the dog does not surrender totally to primordial urges. Considered within the framework of London's socialistic beliefs, communal ties do enrich the individual if they are not carried to the extremes of modern civilization. Thus, the dog's newfound world seems primitive to the reader only in that it is stripped of all civilized pretense.

Jack London's
The Call of the Wild

Raymond Benoit

Raymond Benoit has taught at Saint Louis University. He is the author of Single Nature's Double Name: The Collectedness of the Conflicting in British and American Romanticism.

In agreeing with other critics that pastoralism (country life, particularly that focused on raising and herding livestock) is a driving force in American literature in general, Benoit states that Jack London promotes the simple life in The Call of the Wild. *Benoit argues that London saw the dangers of America's transition from an agrarian nation to an industrial one, and that he favored the former is implicit in Buck's journey back to a simpler, more natural existence. Even the syntactical style that London uses mirrors this theme, Benoit says, as characters such as the brutal trio of Charles, Hal, and Mercedes are described with complex entangled sentences. When Buck is alone, London conversely employs simple, imagistic prose. Like Mark Twain's* The Adventures of Huckleberry Finn *and Henry David Thoreau's* Walden, The Call of the Wild *favors a clean, uncomplicated lifestyle in nature as opposed to the debilitating influence of civilization.*

Enough is known of London's Darwinism [after naturalist Charles Darwin], Nietzscheism [after philosopher Friedrich Nietzsche] and socialism. Not so current, perhaps, is the extent to which his works reflect the pastoral protest that [critic] Mr. John [P.] Sisk finds so pervasive in our literature. In his article, "American Pastoral," Mr. Sisk finds the gist of the pas-

Raymond Benoit, "Jack London's *The Call of the Wild*," *American Quarterly*, vol. 20, no. 2, Part I, Summer 1968, pp. 246–48. Copyright © 1968 by Johns Hopkins University Press. All rights reserved. Reproduced by permission.

toralism [country life, particularly with regard to raising and herding livestock] to be "a critical view of simplicity . . . in context with the non-simple (therefore the less innocent, less wise, less integrated) which it measures. . . . There is always the awareness of an older, debilitated, hopelessly artificial and complex civilization, at once watching with awe and being dramatically criticized and found wanting." London used just this pastoral mode in *The Call of the Wild*: The myth of Buck, the great dog, is an embodiment of the American dream of escaping from the entangling complexity of modern living back to a state as unencumbered as the sled that Buck pulls. Buck, from this angle, is as much an American hero as [American writer Washington Irving's character] Rip Van Winkle—he shakes superfluities from himself. From the moment he learns to dig a hole in the snow to sleep in, all his Southern heritage, the nurture of Santa Clara Valley, begins to fall away:

> The snow walls pressed him on every side, and a great surge of fear swept through him—the fear of the wild thing for the trap. It was a token that he was harking back through his own life to the lives of his forbears; for he was a civilized dog, an unduly civilized dog and of his own experience knew no trap and so could not of himself fear it.

The significant word is "unduly." London's point in this novel and in all his novels is that agrarian America in becoming industrialized had traded the undulations of celestial music, as [American transcendentalist Henry David] Thoreau stated, for factory bells, and had as a consequence lost contact with that saving nature which ultimately mattered. "Much of the old brutal ignorance that had in it also a kind of beautiful childlike innocence is gone forever," [American novelist] Sherwood Anderson lamented in *Winesburg, Ohio*; and in 1920, "Couldn't she somehow, some yet unimagined how," [American novelist] Sinclair Lewis asked of [his character in the novel *Main Street*] Carol Kennicott, "turn it back to simplicity?" The question reverberates with the force of an archetype through our literature, through [American novelist William] Faulkner (*Sartoris*), through [American novelist Ernest] Hemingway (*In Our Time*, especially [in the short story] "Big Two-Hearted River"), and into contemporary American poetry (Robert Bly, James Wright, Gary Snyder). Part of a context, then, the value of *The Call of the Wild* is just that this motif of pastoralism is so very clear in it. Good in its own right, it is a cartoon, in a way, of more major accomplishments. Readily understood, it is an excellent and useful introduction because it hones the point so cleanly that Hemingway and Faulkner, among others, do much more fancy whittling to attain. Not just about a dog, the book is a ritual enactment of the American wish to turn back to simplicity. Buck goes to Alaska and there London reduces life to its lowest terms, discovers under so much complexity what life is essentially all about. Buck in Alaska takes his rightful place among those heroes in American literature who counteract in our imagination, by living more fully, those others we revere for getting ahead, like Spitz the lead dog, "cold and calculating," whom Buck ritually defeats. For from the beginning our worship has been schismatic, Franklins [referring to American politician and inventor Benjamin Franklin] on the one side and Thoreaus on the other, of our twin ideal that the Puritan John Cotton characterized as "diligence in earthly affairs and deadness to the world." There is no doubt where Buck belongs:

> Each day mankind and the claims of mankind slipped farther from him. Deep in the forest a call was sounding, and as often as he heard this call, mysteriously thrilling and luring, he felt compelled to turn his back upon the fire and the beaten earth around it, and to plunge into the forest, and on and on, he knew not where or why; nor did he wonder where or why, the call sounding imperiously, deep in the forest.

The claims of mankind are represented in the novel by Charles, Hal and Mercedes, nature's interlopers in the north to

"The wolf was suspicious and afraid."

Buck encounters a frightened wolf in The Call of the Wild. © Chronicle/Alamy.

whom Buck is sold by Perrault and Francois. Buck had been uneasy during the transaction and his fear is later justified when he first sees the camp of his new owners, "a slipshod and slovenly affair, tent half stretched, dishes unwashed, everything in disorder. . . ." It is the opposite of the clean well-lighted place that Buck's later master and Nature's Nobleman, John Thornton, keeps. Thornton's two partners, Hans and Pete, "were of the same large type as Thornton, living close to the earth, thinking simply and seeing clearly. . . ." Such a pastoral trinity is in meaningful contrast to the wrangling threesome of Charles, Hal and Mercedes "slack in all things, without order or discipline." They are products of artificial and complex civilization and as such are measured by the established norm of simplicity and found hopelessly wanting:

> Starting from a dispute as to which should chop a few sticks for the fire (a dispute which concerned only Charles and Hal), presently would be lugged in the rest of the family, fathers, mothers, uncles, cousins, people thousands of miles away, and some of them dead. That Hal's views on art, or the sort of society plays his mother's brother wrote, should have anything to do with the chopping of a few sticks of firewood, passes comprehension; nevertheless the quarrel was as likely to tend in that direction as in the direction of Charles's political prejudices. And that Charles's sister's talebearing tongue should be relevant to the building of a Yukon fire, was apparent only to Mercedes, who disburdened herself of copious opinions upon that topic, and incidentally upon a few other traits unpleasantly peculiar to her husband's family. In the meantime the fire remained unbuilt, the camp half pitched, and the dogs unfed.

The language itself ("disburdened herself of copious opinions") takes on the messy headiness of abstraction that is the syntactic equivalent of the effete, over-complicated society the book criticizes. The phrases, "sort of society plays his mother's brother wrote" and "Charles's sister's tale-bearing tongue," are a verbal exhibit of civilization's bedeviling complexity; they are onomatopoetic of the sputtering exasperation with which the pastoral writer by definition views such entanglement.

When Buck is the subject, however, the prose moves with his rhythmic gait to the tune of [poet William Carlos Williams's phrase] "no ideas but in things": "Fish, in open pools, were not too quick for him; nor were beaver, mending their dams, too wary."

Characteristically, Charles, Hal and Mercedes overload the sled just as they overload the syntax. The dogs are overworked and clubbed when they become too weak from lack of food to pull the load that civilization demands. Charles, Hal and Mercedes (civilization) fail to pull down their vanity and learn of the green (in this case, white) world; they are judged and condemned by London to a death caused by the weight of their own baggage which cracks the river ice.

By so criticizing society, *The Call of the Wild* is akin to yet another very archetypally American book—*[The Adventures of] Huckleberry Finn* [by Mark Twain]. It also involves a flight for freedom from the debilitating influences of civilization. Like Huck, Buck's been there before and he will never go back. "Simplify, simplify" Thoreau urged; London's prose style communicates this content as much as the content itself. "At home it was all too complicated" says Krebs [in Hemingway's story "Soldier's Home"], one of the first in a long line of Hemingway's pastoral heroes. And like Hemingway's uncomplicated style, clean and well-lighted to both match and be his theme, London's prose opens out to be in structure what it is in theme: like Buck, "free in the open, the unpacked earth underfoot, the wide sky overhead."

Buck Takes a Mythical Journey into the Unknown

Earle Labor and Jeanne Campbell Reesman

Earle Labor has written and edited several books on Jack London and is curator of the Jack London Museum in Shreveport, Louisiana. He is also Wilson Professor of American Literature at Centenary College of Louisiana. Jeanne Campbell Reesman is a professor of English at the University of Texas at San Antonio. Her books include Jack London: One Hundred Years a Writer, Jack London: A Study of the Short Fiction, *and* Jack London, Photographer.

Labor and Reesman view The Call of the Wild *as a journey in the tradition of mythologist Joseph Campbell's delineation of the heroic quest, during which Buck goes through four major stages that transform him from a mundane, everyday canine to a heroic, mythical creature. In the first stage, Buck's initiation, he leaves the domestic world and begins a transformation that carries him "deep into Nature's heart of darkness." In the second, he becomes a hero and leader, but not quite a deific character. The third stage, Buck's rebirth, is spent with his loving owner John Thornton, and in the fourth, Buck fully makes his way into the landscape of myth, running with the wolves. Labor and Reesman see in Buck's transformation a version of every human's wish for individuation and selfhood. In Buck's metamorphosis into fully realized completeness, readers can hear a clear echo of their own deepest desires.*

London said he wrote *The Call of the Wild* to redeem the species [after his negative canine portrayal in his short story "Bâtard"]. "I started it as a companion to my other dog

Earle Labor and Jeanne Campbell Reesman, *Jack London.* United States Authors Series, 1994, 1E., pp. 40–46. Copyright © 1994 Cengage Learning.

story 'Bâtard,' which you may remember; but it got away from me, and instead of 4,000 words it ran 32,000 before I could call a halt." [London's daughter] Joan London tells us that as far as her father was concerned, this masterpiece was "a purely-fortuitous piece of work, a lucky shot in the dark that had unexpectedly found its mark," and that, when reviewers enthusiastically interpreted *The Call of the Wild* as a brilliant human allegory, he was astonished: "'I plead guilty,' he admitted, 'but I was unconscious of it at the time. I did not mean to do it.'" However, he was not entirely oblivious to the story's unusual merit. . . .

Critical Interpretations

[Critic] Maxwell Geismar gives a clue to the deeper layer of meaning when he classifies the work as "a beautiful prose poem, or *nouvelle*, of gold and death on the instinctual level" and as a "handsome parable of the buried impulses." We need only interpolate that these "buried impulses" are essentially human, not canine, and that readers identify more closely than they may realize with this protagonist. The plot is animated by one of the most basic of archetypal motifs: the Myth of the Hero. The call to adventure, departure, initiation, the perilous journey to the mysterious life center, transformation, and apotheosis: These are the phases of the Myth; and all are present in Buck's progress from the civilized world through the natural and beyond to the supernatural world. His journey carries him not only through space but also through time and, ultimately, into the still center of a world that is timeless.

[Critic] Richard Chase points out that in the type of long fiction most properly designated as the *romance*, character becomes "somewhat abstract and ideal," and plot is "highly colored": "Astonishing events may occur, and these are likely to have a symbolic or ideological, rather than a realistic, plausibility. Being less committed to the immediate rendition of reality than the novel, the romance will more freely veer toward mythic, allegorical, and symbolistic forms." All of these remarks are directly applicable to *The Call of the Wild*, in which the richly symbolistic form ultimately becomes the content of the fiction. The seven chapters of the work fall into four major parts or movements. Each of these movements is distinguished by its own theme, rhythm, and tone; each is climaxed by an event of dramatic intensity; and each marks a stage in the hero's transformation from a phenomenal into an ideal figure.

The First Stage in the Hero's Transformation

Part 1, consisting of three chapters, is, with its emphasis on physical violence and amoral survival, the most naturalistic [realistic and factual]—and the most literal—of the book. Its rhythms are quick, fierce, muscular. Images of intense struggle, pain, and blood predominate. Chapter 1, "Into the Primitive," describes the great dog's kidnapping from Judge Miller's pastoral ranch and his subsequent endurance of the first rites of his initiation—the beginning of the transformation that ultimately carries him deep into nature's heart of darkness: "For two days and nights he neither ate nor drank, and during those two days and nights of torment, he accumulated a fund of wrath that boded ill for whoever first fell foul of him. His eyes turned blood-shot, and he was metamorphosed into a raging fiend. So changed was he that the Judge himself would not have recognized him; and the express messengers breathed with relief when they bundled him off the train at Seattle."

The high priest of Buck's first initiatory rites is the symbolic figure in the red sweater, the man with the club who relentlessly pounds the hero into a disciplined submission to the code of violence and toil. "Well, Buck, my boy," the man calmly observes after the merciless beating, "we've had our little ruction, and the best thing we can do is to let it go at that. You've learned your place, and I know mine." Like all of London's heroes who survive the rigors of the White Silence, Buck has passed the first test: that of adaptability.

Chapter 2, "The Law of Club and Fang," takes the hero to the northland. On Dyea Beach he encounters the dogs and men who are to become his traveling companions in the long, hard months ahead. He also continues to absorb the lessons of survival. Curly, the most amiable of the newly arrived pack, is knocked down by a veteran husky, then ripped apart by the hordes of canine spectators. The scene remains vividly etched in Buck's memory: "So that was the way. No fair play. Once down, that was the end of you." Later, as he is broken into his traces for the trail, he awakens to the great driving motivation of the veteran sled dogs: the extraordinary love of toil. But more significant is the metamorphosis of his moral values. He learns, for example, that stealing, an unthinkable misdeed in his former state, can be the difference between survival and death: "It was all well enough in the Southland, under the law of love and fellowship, to respect private property and personal feelings; but in the Northland, under the law of club and fang, whoso took such things into account was a fool, and in so far as he observed them he would fail to prosper."

Chapter 3, "The Dominant Primordial Beast," marks the conclusion of the first major phase of Buck's initiation, for it reveals that he is not merely qualified as a member of the pack but that he is worthy of leadership. This chapter has a pronounced modulation of style to signal the glimmerings of Buck's mythic destiny; instead of sharply detailed physical description, we begin to encounter passages of tone poetry:

> With the aurora borealis flaming coldly overhead, or the stars leaping in the frost dance, and the land numb and frozen under its pall of snow, this song of the huskies might have been the defiance of life, only it was pitched in minor key, with long-drawn wailings and half-sobs, and was more the pleading of life, the articulate travail of existence. When

'Pitched in minor key, with long-drawn wailings and half sobs.''

Buck and his pack of huskies howl under the aurora borealis in The Call of the Wild. © Mary Evans Picture Library/Alamy.

he moaned and sobbed, it was with the pain of living that was of old the pain of his wild fathers, and the fear and mystery of the cold and dark that was to them fear and mystery.

London's style becomes increasingly lyrical as the narrative rises from literal to symbolic level, and it reaches such intensity near the end of chapter 3 that we now realize Buck's is no common animal story:

> There is an ecstasy that marks the summit of life, and beyond which life cannot rise. And such is the paradox of living, this ecstasy comes when one is most alive, and it comes as a complete forgetfulness that one is alive. This ecstasy, this forgetfulness of living, comes to the artist, caught up and out of himself in a sheet of flame; it comes to the soldier, war-mad on a stricken field and refusing quarter; and it came to Buck, leading the pack, sounding the old wolf-cry, straining after the food that was alive and that fled swiftly before him through the moonlight. He was sounding the deeps of his nature, and of the parts of his nature that were deeper than he, going back into the womb of Time. He was mastered by the sheen surging of life, the tidal wave of being, the perfect joy of each separate muscle, joint, and sinew in that it was everything that was not death, that it was aglow and rampant, expressing itself in movement, flying exultantly under the stars and over the face of dead matter that did not move.

This paragraph is a thematic epitome of the whole work, and it functions as a prologue to the weird moonlit scene in which Buck challenges Spitz for leadership of the team. . . .

The Second Stage in Buck's Hero Journey

Even though Buck has now "Won to Mastership" (chapter 4), he is not ready for apotheosis. He is a leader and a hero—but he is not yet a god. His divinity must be confirmed, as prescribed by ritual, through death and rebirth. After the climactic pulsations of chapter 3, a slowing of beat occurs in the second movement. Death occurs symbolically, almost literally, in chapter 5 ("The Toil of Trace and Trail"). Clustering darkly, the dominant images are those of pain and fatigue as Buck and his teammates suffer under the ownership of the three *chechaquos* [newcomers]: Charles, his wife Mercedes, and her brother Hal—"a nice family party." Like the two Incapables of "In a Far Country," they display all the fatal symptoms of incompetence and unfitness: "Buck felt vaguely that there was no depending upon these two men and the woman. They did not know how to do anything, and as days went by it became apparent that they could not learn. They were slack in all things, without order or discipline." Without a sense of economy or the will to work and endure hardship themselves, they overwork, starve, and beat their dogs—then they turn on one another:

> Their irritability arose out of their misery, increased with it, doubled upon it, outdistanced it. The wonderful patience of the trail which comes to all men who toil hard and suffer sore, and remain sweet of speech and kindly, did not come to these two men and the woman. They had no inkling of such a patience. They were stiff and in pain; their muscles ached, their bones ached, their very hearts ached; and because of this they became sharp of speech, and hard words were first on their lips in the morning and last at night.

This ordeal is the second long and difficult phase of Buck's initiation. The "long journey" is described in increasingly morbid imagery as the "perambulating skeletons" and "wayfarers of death" approach closer to their fatal end in the thawing ice of the Yukon River; the journey ends with Buck's symbolic crucifixion as he is beaten nearly to death by Hal shortly before the ghostly caravan moves on without him and disappears into the icy maw of the river.

Third and Forth Stages

Buck's rebirth comes in chapter 6, "For the Love of Man," which also functions as the third and transitional movement of the narrative. Having been rescued by John Thornton, the benign helper who traditionally appears in the Myth to lead the hero toward his goal, Buck is now being readied for the final phase of his odyssey. Appropriately, the season is spring; and the mood is idyllic as he wins back his strength, "lying by the river bank through the long spring days, watching the running water, listening lazily to the songs of the birds and the hum of nature. . . ." And, during this same convalescent period, the hints of his destiny grow more insistent: "He was older than the days he had seen and the breaths he had drawn. He linked the past with the present, and the eternity behind him throbbed through him in a mighty rhythm to which he swayed as the tides and seasons swayed. . . . Deep in the forest a call was sounding. . . . But as often as he gained the soft unbroken earth and the green shade, the love for John Thornton drew him back. . . ." The passionate devotion of Thornton climaxes in the final scene of chapter 6 when Buck wins a $1,000 wager for his master by moving a half-ton sled 100 yards; this legendary feat, which concludes the third movement of the narrative, foreshadows the hero's supernatural appointment in the fourth and final movement.

Chapter 7, "The Sounding of the Call," consummates Buck's transformation. In keeping with this change, London shifts both the setting and the tone. Thornton, taking the money earned by Buck in the wager, begins his last quest "into the East after a fabled lost mine, the history of which was as old as the history of the country . . . steeped in tragedy and shrouded in mystery." As the small party moves into the wilderness, the scene assumes a mythic atmosphere and the caravan is enveloped in a strange aura of timelessness:

> The months came and went, and back and forth they twisted through the uncharted vastness, where no men were and yet where men had been if the Lost Cabin were true. They went across divides in summer blizzards, shivered under the midnight sun on naked mountains between the timber line and

the eternal snows, dropped into summer valleys amid swarming gnats and flies, and in the shadows of glaciers picked strawberries and flowers as ripe and fair as any the Southland could boast. In the fall of the year they penetrated a weird lake country, sad and silent, where wild-fowl had been, but where then there was no life nor sign of life— only the blowing chill winds, the forming of ice in sheltered places, and the melancholy rippling of waves on lonely beaches.

Into the Unknown

The weirdness of the atmosphere is part of the "call to adventure" described by [American mythologist] Joseph Campbell in *The Hero with a Thousand Faces*, which "signifies that destiny has summoned the hero and transferred his spiritual center of gravity from within the pale of society to a zone unknown. This fateful region of both treasure and danger may be variously represented: as a distant land, a forest, . . . or profound dream state; but it is always a place of strangely fluid and polymorphous beings, unimaginable torments, superhuman deeds and impossible delight." This "fateful region of both treasure and danger" is a far cry from Judge Miller's pastoral ranch and from the raw frontier of the Klondike gold rush: It is the landscape of myth. The party finally arrives at its destination, a mysterious and incredibly rich placer valley where "like giants they toiled, days flashing on the heels of days like dreams as they heaped the treasure up."

His role fulfilled as guide into the unknown zone, Thornton and his party are killed by the savage Yeehats, and Buck is released from the bond of love to fulfill the last phase of his apotheosis as he is transformed into the immortal Ghost Dog of Northland legend. He incarnates the eternal mystery of creation and life: "[And when] the long winter nights come on and the wolves follow their meat into the lower valleys . . . a great, gloriously coated wolf, like, and yet unlike, all other wolves . . . may be seen running at the head of the pack through the pale moonlight or glimmering borealis, leaping gigantic above his fellows, his great throat abellow as he sings a song of the younger world, which is the song of the pack."

Although *The Call of the Wild* was perhaps no luckier than any other great artistic achievement, it was "a shot in the dark" in an unintended sense—into the dark wilderness of the unconscious. And as with other great literary works, its ultimate meaning eludes us. But at least a significant part of that meaning relates to the area of human experience that cannot be translated into discursive terms and that must therefore be approached tentatively and obliquely. After granting this much, we may infer that the animating force of London's wild romance is the vital energy [Swiss psychiatrist Carl] Jung called *libido* and that London's hero is a projection of the reader's own *self* eternally striving for psychic integration in the process called *individuation* [development of the individual]. Such an inference accounts for the appropriateness of London's division of his narrative into seven chapters that fall naturally into four movements, quaternity symbolizing, in Jung's words, "the ideal of completeness" and "the totality of the personality," and seven, the archetypal number of perfect order and the consummation of a cycle. But, of course, we do not need such a technical explanation to know that the call to which we respond as the great Ghost Dog flashes through the glimmering borealis singing his song of the younger world is the faint but clear echo of a music deep within ourselves.

Buck Escapes the Capitalist System by Returning to the Wild

Gina M. Rossetti

Gina M. Rossetti is an assistant professor of English at Saint Xavier University in Chicago, Illinois. Her research and pedagogical interests lie in American literary naturalism, and in particular Jack London's work.

Contesting the more prevalent reading of The Call of the Wild *as a Darwinian statement, Rossetti instead argues that Jack London was writing a "socialist folktale." Buck's journey into the wild is a movement away from American capitalism, where he is owned by men, to a more primitive, new, and improved society. For Rossetti, the novel's "labor crisis" presents itself in three important symbolic scenes: Curly's death, Buck's thievery, and Buck's challenge to Spitz. These scenes show the power owners have over workers and the lengths to which workers are pushed to survive in a capitalist system. Buck's story repudiates the system that forces him into servile labor at the same time as it points to a socialist utopia where workers can live freely.*

London begins *The Call of the Wild* with an epigraph from John [Myers] O'Hara's poem "Atavism": "Old longings nomadic leap, / Chafing at custom's chain; / Again from its brumal sleep / Wakens the ferine strain." As the lines suggest, the story that unfolds focuses on the "natural" reawakening of dormant passions. Immediately complicating this epigraph,

Gina M. Rossetti, *Imagining the Primitive in Naturalist and Modernist Literature.* Columbia: University of Missouri Press, 2006, pp. 30–35. Reprinted by permission of the University of Missouri Press. Copyright ©2006 by the Curators of the University of Missouri.

however, is the discovery of gold, which is revealed in the novel's opening sentences, a discovery that triggers Buck's kidnapping and forced labor. From the novel's beginning, one observes the tension between the "survival of the fittest" and anticapitalist rhetoric. Significantly, the culture's valuation of gold, not Buck's innate wildness per se, plunges him into the primitive as a laborer in the gold rush. Sold initially to a dog breaker referred to as "the man in the red sweater," Buck not only learns how to defer to men but he also observes the money transactions between unknown men and the man in the red sweater: "Now and again men came, strangers, who talked excitedly, wheedlingly, and in all kinds of fashions to the man in the red sweater. And at such times that money passed between them the strangers took one or more of the dogs away with them. Buck wondered where they went, for they never came back; but the fear of the future was strong upon him, and he was glad each time when he was not selected." Eventually, Buck is sold to two representatives from the Canadian government, Francois and Perrault, who need the dogs to deliver dispatches reporting on the status of the gold rush. Buck's first owners thus subject him to forced labor, a pattern that will repeat throughout much of the novel.

A Critique of Capitalist Labor

The novel's labor crisis and the culture it breeds present themselves in three key moments: Curly's death, Buck's thievery, and Buck's challenge to Spitz. Buck's never-ending labor is underscored by Perrault's desire to shatter records in their travels to Dawson in order to exchange information about gold finds that will benefit the Canadian government. One learns that Perrault, "as [a] courier for the Canadian government, bearing important despatches, was anxious to secure the best dogs." This new environment fosters action, alert behavior, and ruthlessness. As a result, Curly, the only female dog, and her humane disposition are out of place in the Klondike, and the other dogs target her for their barbarism. Curly's death scene, in which "[the huskies] closed in upon her, snarling and yelping, and she was buried screaming with agony, beneath the bristling mass of bodies," is emblematic of the labor relations of this environment. Unable to foster community, the dogs turn on one another in a "rooting out" of rival competitors. Witnessing Curly's death, Buck learns that fairness and equity are not transcendent values in the gold rush's brutal economic environment, and "once down, that was the end of you. Well, he would see to it that he never went down."

Buck's new education and his environment's lack of equity reveal themselves further with his pilfering of food. The narrator notes that Buck steals the food not because he is hungry but because "it was easier to do [this] than not to do [it]." The narrator also suggests that Buck's thievery "marked further the decay or going to pieces of his moral nature, a vain thing and a handicap in the ruthless struggle for existence." In separate analyses, [critics] A. Paul Reed and Michael Kumin cite this line as an example of the novel's Darwinian [after naturalist Charles Darwin] "survival of the fittest" argument. However, Buck's "ruthless struggle for existence" might also suggest his economic situation rather than his perceived atavism [primitivism]. Indeed, London maps his critique of capitalist labor practices onto an atavistic moment in order to reveal the depraved acts that this economic system encourages in those at the bottom. While focusing on the professionalization of writing in the novel rather than a socialist critique, [critic] Jonathan Auerbach notes that "the central paradox informing the narrative is that Buck must learn to be wild. Wildness in the book . . . entails disciplined education." To focus on Buck's regression as a moral critique rather than as an economic one overlooks his position as a pawn in a much larger economic system. Buck's thievery and Curly's death suggest that those who do not control their own labor must commit acts of aggression against those who control the workers' labor and subsistence; failing to do this, one falls victim to the savagery that marks this depraved environment.

Buck's ruthless environment, coupled with its emphasis on competition, manifests itself further in his challenge for Spitz's lead-dog position. Just as Perrault attempts to outperform other government couriers, so, too, does Buck challenge Spitz's dominance. Indeed, Buck's challenge is rendered in human terms as the narrator notes that "all that stirring of old instincts . . . [which] drives men out from the sounding cities to forest and plain to kill things by chemically propelled leaden pellets, the blood lust, the joy to kill—all this was Buck's." While Spitz is the more experienced fighting dog, his superior track record proves futile against Buck's spirit. As they fight, "the silent and wolfish circle waited to finish off whichever dog went down." The fighting dogs and the expectant hungry pack render the brutality "natural," and while this supports a Darwinian enactment of the survival of the fittest, dominance in this novel is also characterized in real labor and economic terms. At the fight's conclusion, when "Buck stood and looked on, the successful champion, the dominant primordial beast who had made his kill and found it good," his victory underscores the breakdown of community and the ruthless and rugged individualism that are needed in Buck's brutal capitalist environment.

Poor Labor Management vs. an Ideal Owner

These incidents, along with his sale to another gold rush owner, mark Buck's degraded labor environment. In the chapter entitled "The Toil of Trace and Trail," Buck is sold once again, this time to three neophytes [newcomers] whose ignorance about the Klondike and reckless pursuit of a gold mine windfall mark his and the other dogs' further victimization. One learns immediately about Hal's, Charles's, and Mercedes's inexperience, and their reckless pursuit of gold reveals their indifference to the dogs' sacrifices. For instance, Mercedes's willful helplessness underscores her profound indifference to real workers' plights. The narrator notes that "it was her custom to be helpless. . . . She no longer considered the dogs, and because she was sore and tired, she persisted in riding on the sled. She was pretty and soft, but she weighed one hundred and twenty pounds—a lusty last straw to the load dragged by the weak and starving animals." Ignoring the advice from experienced Klondike men, Hal believes that the dogs' unwillingness to pull the sled shows that "you've got to whip them to get anything out of them. That's their way." However, John Thornton immediately refutes this conclusion and notes that the dogs' unrelenting labor, heavy load, and systematic starving are the reasons behind their refusal to work. Frustrated by their own incompetence, Hal, Charles, and Mercedes punish the dogs for their own failures and deprive them of food. London ironically notes that "it was a simple matter to give the dogs less food; but it was impossible to make the dogs travel faster, while their own inability to get under way earlier in the morning prevented them from travelling longer hours. Not only did they not know how to work the dogs, but they did not know how to work themselves." This depiction of the three neophytes, and their eventual fall through the ice, suggests that the bourgeoisie are unable to manage labor, are ignorant to the workers' problems, and contribute willfully to the workers' degradation, all of which eventually lead to their own and the workers' destruction.

In marked contrast to Mercedes, Hal, and Charles, John Thornton is regarded as the ideal owner, whose kind treatment of Buck bespeaks an enlightened attitude toward labor. Many moments support this romantic depiction of Thornton, such as his rescue of Buck from the abusive neophytes, his uncanny rapport with and momentary "taming" of Buck, and his insistence on rest for his dogs. However, this romantic picture is undermined by his wager for money on Buck's labor

"John Thornton and Buck looked at each other."

Buck and his master John Thornton in The Call of the Wild. © Susan Isakson/Alamy.

and his tricks against Buck to prove to others his dog's un-
thinking devotion to him. These incidents underscore that

even with Thornton, Buck still does not own his own labor. While Thornton may act more kindly in his overall treatment of Buck, he owns his labor and uses him to uncover an ancient and rumored gold mine.

A Socialist Folktale

The novel's continual emphasis on the dogs' labor suggests that its focus on primitivism is a starting point for its socialist critique of capitalism, and Buck's removal to the wild lays the groundwork for a socialist folktale. That is, in escaping from man-centered society, Buck not only takes back his labor but also returns to a "younger world," the same world that has been the subject of his numerous dreams. In his dreams, Buck's younger world, one that is much like the one depicted in the later London novel *Before Adam*, has many atavistic features that remind Buck of his ancient heritage of wild dogs and that tell him this environment, rather than the one populated by modern men, is his natural home: "Each day mankind and the claims of mankind slipped farther from him. Deep in the forest a call was sounding, and as often as he heard this call, mysteriously thrilling and luring, he felt compelled to turn his back upon the fire and the beaten earth around it, and to plunge into the forest!" This yearning for the "younger world" is underscored by his "reunion" with his natural wild brother in the woods, and his ecstasy with this new life occurs, rather interestingly, at the moment when Thornton is murdered by the Yeehats. At key moments when Buck becomes an instrument for profit, he is plagued by a series of dreams that bring him back to the "younger world" or pre-capitalist tribal community. On the one hand, these dreams might suggest Buck's natural inclination toward atavistic qualities. On the other hand, it might also suggest that Buck rejects his present condition wherein he does not own his labor. Hence, Buck's adaptation to the northland marks not his acquiescence to a Darwinian "survival of the fittest" scenario but his rejection of forced labor. His return to the wild chronicles, then, an alternative space to capitalism.

One problematizing moment in this socialist folktale, however, is that this alternative world is not utopic; while this life is one wherein Buck no longer works in service to man, it is a world still marked by rank, order, and fear. Indeed, this ranking system manifests itself in this world's obsession with racial memory and the displacement of the Yeehat Native American tribe, acts that fit too comfortably into London's own problematic race theories. Some critics such as A. Paul Reed, Michael Kumin, and Charles Child Walcutt romanticize Buck's murder of the Yeehats because they consider it Buck's revenge against those who murdered Thornton. I would suggest, however, that the murder of these (pre)men represents a dangerous quality in this younger world, one that is already marked by the prejudices and hierarchies that dominate the civilized world. His murder of the Yeehats reveals that Buck adheres to a false consciousness and that these men are further displaced in Buck's return to a pre-capitalist community. That is, the Yeehats' erasure suggests that they, unlike the dog, do not have a mythic homeland that marks their rightful ancestral heritage. Moreover, this younger world's culture of fear suggests that Buck's existence will be one in which he must battle enemies constantly to maintain his dominance, a situation that appears unchanged from that in the "civilized" world he left.

In *The Call of the Wild*, the problematic combination of three foci about primitivism mark the novel's key conflicts. While many critics note its indebtedness to a Darwinian survival of the fittest scenario, the novel also points to a socialist critique of labor combined with a racialist dream for this "new and improved" society. Nowhere in the text does Buck emerge as one who possesses a "revolutionary" consciousness because even in the younger world he acts according to the dictates of the civilized world. Moreover, the socialist utopia that should mark this younger world is not present as this world still maintains a rank-ordered society as governed by the wolf community. When Buck "sings a song of the younger world, which is the song of the pack," he perpetuates a divided dream, a dream that on the one hand repudiates the enforced and degraded labor of the novel's hero, and on the other hand, continues to point to a kind of rightful place for the chosen people in which their preeminence can be reinstated.

The Call of the Wild Is a Study in Devolution

Jacqueline Tavernier-Courbin

Jacqueline Tavernier-Courbin is a professor of English at the University of Ottawa in Canada. Her books include Ernest Hemingway's A Moveable Feast: The Making of Myth *and* Critical Essays on Jack London.

Tavernier-Courbin focuses on the naturalistic elements in The Call of the Wild. *Literary naturalism is the idea that humans are subject to heredity, environment, and social conditions and that their lives are largely determined by these forces. Tavernier-Courbin asserts that* The Call of the Wild *primarily traces what happens to a beast when its environment changes and it must adapt to survive. Buck's metamorphosis necessarily entails his devolution into an amoral character, one who will do whatever is necessary to adapt to the northern wilderness and the harshness of life there. For London, Tavernier-Courbin suggests, this descent into amorality contradicts the moral qualities his heroic characters need to develop in order to survive.*

The influence of heredity and the milieu, the concept of the survival of the fittest and adaptation as the key to survival are overwhelmingly important in *The Call of the Wild*. The book deals less with the concept of evolution than with that of devolution—the return to the primitive of a civilized being when his environment has changed from one of mellow civilization to one of brutality where the only law is eat or be eaten, kill or be killed.

Early Lessons

Until he is kidnapped, Buck has lived the life of a sated aristocrat, king over "all creeping, crawling, flying things of Judge

Jacqueline Tavernier-Courbin, *The Call of the Wild: A Naturalistic Romance.* EBK: CALL OF THE WILD, 1E., pp. 56–62. Copyright © 1995 Cengage Learning.

Miller's place, humans included." His education into the harsh realities of an unprotected life begins shortly after he is abducted, and after a two-day-and-night train journey during which he was vilely treated and neither ate nor drank. After having changed hands several times and in a fever of pain and rage, Buck meets the man in the red sweater who is the first step of his initiation into the wild: the dog breaker. Buck had never been struck with a club in his life, but again and again with each new charge he is brought crushingly to the ground by a vicious blow of the club. Although his rage knows no bounds and although he is a large, powerful dog, he is no match against a man who is "no slouch at dog-breakin'" and knows how to handle a club efficiently. The man in the red sweater finishes Buck with a blow directly on the nose and a final "shrewd blow" that knocks him unconscious. Buck thus learns his first lesson: that a man with a club is a master to be obeyed, although not necessarily conciliated. "That club was a revelation. It was his introduction to the reign of primitive law, and he met the introduction half-way." Buck, however, retains his dignity and never fawns on his masters. They are stronger than he is; therefore, in order to survive, he obeys them. Having seen a dog who would neither obey nor conciliate killed in the struggle for mastery made the alternatives clear to him: to obey, to conciliate, or to die. The lesson is enforced each time Buck watches another dog being broken. A survivor above all else, Buck knows he is beaten, but his spirit is never broken.

Buck's next lesson takes place on Dyea Beach when Curly, whom he has befriended, is killed by the huskies when she makes advances to one of them in her usual friendly way. In two minutes, she is literally torn to pieces. "So that was the way. No fair play. Once down, that was the end of you. Well [Buck] would see to it that he never went down." This traumatic lesson often returns to haunt Buck's sleep. There seems to be only one law in this new world that both men and beasts obey—the law of club and fang—and like Dave and Sol-leks, one has to learn to give nothing, ask for nothing, and expect nothing.

Adapting to a new environment also entails learning other lessons, not only simple lessons such as digging a hole in the snow to sleep in or eating quickly to leave no one the time to steal his food, but also lessons involving moral changes. Buck learns to steal, and London makes it clear that his first theft marked Buck as fit to survive in the hostile northland environment. "It marked his adaptability, his capacity to adjust himself to changing conditions, the lack of which would have meant swift and terrible death. It marked, further, the decay or going to pieces of his moral nature, a vain thing and a handicap in the ruthless struggle for existence." London comments with some irony that, while living on Judge Miller's estate, Buck would have died for a moral principle, such as the defense of the Judge's riding whip, but that "the completeness of his decivilization was now evidenced by his ability to flee from the defense of a moral consideration and so save his hide." Among other moral qualities Buck sheds are his sense of fair play and of mercy, which are things reserved for gentler climates. In the wilderness of the north, survival is the only goal and ruthlessness the only way to survive. Thus, Buck learns through experience and proves that he is eminently adaptable and fit. His body also adapts well to the new demands of the environment: He loses his fastidiousness, grows callous to pain, achieves an internal as well as an external economy, making the most of whatever comes his way, his senses develop to an incredible acuteness, and forgotten instincts come to life in him. Indeed, heredity also plays an important role in his survival:

> And not only did he learn by experience, but instincts long dead became alive again. The domesticated generations fell from him. In vague ways he remembered back to the youth of the breed, to the time the wild dogs ranged in packs

through the primeval forest and killed their meat as they ran it down. It was no task for him to learn to fight with cut and slash and the quick wolf snap. In this manner had fought forgotten ancestors. They quickened the old life within him, and the old tricks which they had stamped into the heredity of the breed were his tricks. They came to him without effort or discovery, as though they had been his always.

This link with a remote past when men and dogs were wild is the major theme running throughout the book and is handled by London not only as a naturalistic [in which harsh realities are exposed] theme but also as a mythical and archetypal [referring to ancient patterns] one.

The Instinct to Kill

Since the wolf is a predator, the basic instinct coming to life in Buck is the instinct to kill—an instinct of which he was not originally conscious. He progresses fast, beginning with small game and, eventually, killing man. The instinct to kill, as London makes clear, is common to all predators, and man himself has not completely lost it and indulges it when he goes shooting or hunting. However, for Buck, the killing is infinitely more intimate because it is not carried out by proxy through a bullet: "He was ranging at the head of the pack, running the wild thing down, the living meat, to kill with his own teeth and wash his muzzle to the eyes in warm blood." Although it is Spitz, instead of Buck, who kills the snowshoe rabbit, its death marks the awakening of Buck's own desire to kill, and he immediately challenges Spitz to a fight to the death—a fight Buck wins largely because the knowledge of ancestral fighting techniques becomes his instantly: "As they circled about, snarling, ears laid back, keenly watchful for the advantage, the scene came to Buck with a sense of familiarity. He seemed to remember it all—the white woods, and earth, and moonlight, and the thrill of battle. . . . To Buck it was nothing new or strange, this scene of old time. It was as though it had always been, the wonted way of things." After defeating Spitz, and while the pack has closed in upon his crippled enemy, "Buck stood and looked on, the successful champion, the dominant primordial beast who had made his kill and found it good." Buck has indeed now come of age, and although his education is not finished, he has proven that he is one of the fit.

Once Buck has proven himself on the hereditary and environmental levels and has reverted to instinctual patterns of behavior, his life with a new master, John Thornton, suddenly becomes more mellow and affords him the opportunity to relax his vigilance. But Buck cannot return to his old self, for he has learned only too well the lessons of the wild—that one should never forgo an advantage or draw back from a fight one has started, that mercy is misunderstood for fear or weakness, and that such misunderstanding makes for death. He has gained knowledge from the depth of time, and such knowledge cannot be discarded once it has become part of the conscious self. Thus, his life with John Thornton, which could, in other circumstances, have heralded a return to the tame, is merely an interval in Buck's evolution, and the call of the wild keeps summoning him until he has returned fully to the life of his ancestors, until he has become part of nature.

Realistic Depictions

In the last stages of Buck's evolution or devolution, London's handling of the theme of heredity becomes more and more mythical and archetypal. As the "blood longing" becomes stronger in him, Buck fights larger and larger prey and begins to look more and more like his wild brothers, transforming himself in the secrecy of the forest into a thing of the wild, "stealing along softly, cat-footed, a passing shadow that appeared and disappeared among the shadows." Buck kills a large black bear and a huge bull moose he stalks and worries for four days before finally pulling him down with the dogged, tireless, persistent patience of the wild when it hunts its living food. Then, out of despair and anger at the murder of John Thornton, Buck attacks and kills men—the Yeehats who have massacred Thornton's party—kills them in the face of the law of club and fang. His last ties with mankind being broken, Buck is now free to join and lead a pack of wolves and live the life of the wild to the fullest.

From the standpoints of documentation and major themes, *The Call of the Wild* is indeed a naturalistic novel [one that realistically captures nature, both good and bad]. According to the criteria of noninvolvement and objectivity, the story is still rather naturalistic; but in the areas of amorality and rejection of social taboos it is naturalistic by default, for Buck's gorgeous coat of fur allows London to deal uninhibitedly with themes he would otherwise shun. Indeed, many painful and shocking scenes are described by London with perfect objectivity. Among such scenes is the potentially heartrending scene in which Buck is beaten by the man in the red sweater, which is rendered in detail but with no expression of sympathy or pity on London's part. Nor does London dwell on Buck's pain. He merely describes accurately what the man does to Buck and how Buck reacts. The fight between Buck and Spitz, the death of Dave, the stalking and the killing of the bull moose, Buck's standing off the wolf pack are all scenes London handles with perfect objectivity, never indulging in expressions of emotion or pity. He even indicates with remarkable simplicity the economy-of-pain principle upon which the moose herd functions, and how they are ready to pay the price of one head so that the herd might be freed from Buck's menacing presence: "Besides, it was not the life of the herd, or of the young bulls, that was threatened. The life of only one member was demanded, which was a remoter interest in their lives, and in the end they were content to pay the toll."

Pain, suffering, and death, London can describe unemotionally. Love, however, is another matter, but Buck's furry nature allows London not to wax romantic. Although he describes Buck's passionate devotion to John Thornton in abstract terms, he never allows Buck to lose his dignity and fawn upon his master as the other dogs do. The various instances when Buck proves his love for his master, whether it be by attempting to jump over a chasm (which would have been certain death), by attacking "Black" Burton, by risking his own life repeatedly in the rapids to save Thornton's, or, finally, by pulling a sleigh loaded with 1,000 pounds of flour, are always described with a great economy of emotion. London merely describes Buck's actions; love in action, not as an emotion. What expression of feeling London dramatizes is on the part of Thornton. Indeed, the men are awed by the length to which Buck will carry his devotion to Thornton, and Thornton is the one who expresses his love for Buck after the latter has won his bet for him. "Thornton fell on his knees beside Buck. Head was against head, and he was shaking him back and forth. Those who hurried up heard him cursing Buck, and he cursed him long and fervently, and softly and lovingly." The amoral stance of the novel is an easy one for London to carry out since the perfect logic of Buck's reversal to the wild is easily acceptable on the part of an animal. It would be far more difficult to accept on the part of a human being, especially by London's early twentieth-century audience. The needs of the poor young American girls who must not be shocked tend to limit the naturalistic point of view of many of his stories dealing with human protagonists, and many of the themes London dramatizes easily in *The Call of the Wild* are present but transformed in his other fiction. While we are ready to accept Buck's loss of moral principles as a necessary part of his survival, it would be more difficult to do so if Buck were a human protagonist, and London never condones it for his two-legged characters. In fact, in his stories of the north, survival for man calls for virtues such as courage, integrity, and brotherhood. Like dogs, men must change both physically and morally since only the strong shall survive; but they must change for the better morally as well as physically, and, as London makes clear in stories such as "In a Far Country," they must substitute for the courtesies of ordinary life "unselfishness, forbearance, and tolerance." Those who fail usually die a useless and shameful death, after having lived without dignity, such as the protagonists of "In a Far Country" and the miserably incompetent Hal, Charles, and Mercedes in *The Call of the Wild*, who neither "toil hard, suffer sore, and remain sweet of speech and kindly." Indeed, they embody the very antithesis of what man should be in the wilderness of the north if he is to survive. London's ideal hero of [his short story collections] *The Son of the Wolf* and *The God of His Fathers*, Malemute Kid, resembles John Thornton in most ways. Unlike Buck, these men have not lost their moral nature.

Jack London: The Problem of Form

Donald Pizer

Donald Pizer taught English at Tulane University. His books include The Novels of Frank Norris *and* Twentieth-Century American Literary Naturalism: An Interpretation.

In the following viewpoint, Pizer suggests that readers of The Call of the Wild *are off base when they attack London as a false realist, as President Theodore Roosevelt famously did.* The Call of the Wild *is a fable, Pizer suggests, in agreeing with critic Earle Labor that the appeal of London's dog stories is that they are beast fables in which the primordial strength of their animal heroes resonates with readers. Pizer believes that the reason* The Call of the Wild *is usually seen as a better story than its companion,* White Fang, *is because the account of a return to the primitive is more attractive to readers' unconscious desires than White Fang's advance into civilization.* The Call of the Wild *celebrates primal power in a world where power becomes destiny.*

Most of the significant criticism of Jack London has been devoted to two interrelated issues: Is there a coherent center to London's ideas or are they indeed hopelessly confused and contradictory; and what are the sources of London's strength and appeal as a writer given the superficiality of much of his work? So, for example, critics have often grappled with the relationship between London's socialism and Nietzscheism [after German philosopher Friedrich Nietzsche], and they have sought to explain how a writer who could achieve the seamless perfection of [London's short story] "To

Donald Pizer, "Chapter 15, Jack London: The Problem of Form," *Realism and Naturalism in Nineteenth-Century American Literature*. Carbondale: Southern Illinois University Press, 1966, pp. 166–72. Copyright © 1966 by Studies in the Literary Imagination. All rights reserved. Reproduced by permission.

Build a Fire" could also produce an extraordinary amount of trash. Whatever the value of these efforts, almost all have been piecemeal in character. The critic tackles a particular narrow problem or a specific work and then extrapolates from it. At the considerable risk of moving to the other extreme of over-schematization and overgeneralization, I would like to suggest a single dominant solution to the enigma which is Jack London. The notion which I propose to pursue is that London as a thinker and as an artist is essentially a writer of fables and parables.

To help clear the ground, I should note that I do not maintain that there is a clear distinction between the fable and the parable.[1] Both forms are didactic. They seek to establish the validity of a particular moral truth by offering a brief story in which plot, character, and setting are allegorical agents of a paraphrasable moral. But historically, because of the association of fable with [ancient Greek fabulist] Aesop and of parable with the Bible, each of the terms also has a more specialized coloration. By fable is usually meant a work in which beasts (and occasionally inanimate objects) both speak and represent human qualities, and by parable is meant a work in which the principal agents are human. Furthermore, the moral of a fable is apt to be far more worldly than that of a parable. Fables deal with how men act on earth, parables with how they should act to gain salvation.

Fables and parables are not fiction in our modern sense of the distinctive nature of fiction. They simplify experience into useable precept rather than render it as either complex or ambivalent. But in that simplification lies a potential for artistic strength if artistry in this instance can be said to be the restatement in pleasing form of what we as a race or society wish to hear about ourselves. The special appeal of the beast fable is that it substitutes wit for insight; it expresses not deep or fresh perception but rather a concise and clever recapitulation of what everybody knows. In the beast fable, foxes are always shrewd, lions bold, hawks predatory, sheep silly, asses stupid, and so on. Setting is nonexistent or minimal and when present is a condition of the moral dilemma in which the beasts find themselves (a forest is danger, a barn safety). And action is limited to that which renders immediately and clearly the heart of the precept.

Much of the attraction of the fable lies not only in our pleasure in finding clearly recognizable human characteristics confirmed in animals but in the nature of the precepts which these characteristics advance. For the wisdom of the fable is the ancient wisdom of the world—that the shrewd and strong prevail unless blinded by pride, that greed is a great equalizer, and so on. The lesson of the fable is that the world is a place of seeking and grasping in which specific qualities of human nature always receive their just dessert. In the fable, vanity is always victimized by shrewdness, disappointment always seeks rationalization, and desire for gain guides all life.

Parable often moves beyond the way we are to the way we should be. While the precept of a fable is both concrete and expedient (be less vain and you shall prosper more), that of a parable tends toward moral abstractions (be charitable and you will be a better person). And since the ability to frame and respond to moral abstractions is a distinctively human attribute, the personae in a parable are almost always human.

By the late nineteenth century, whatever lines of demarcation that might have existed earlier between fable and parable had for the most part disappeared. In [English writer Rudyard] Kipling's *The Jungle Book*, for example, the worldliness of the beast fable and the more programmatic moralism of the parable join in clear allegories containing both animal and human characters. It was to this blending of the fable/parable form that London was powerfully drawn.

It seems strange today that the principal critical issue for many early readers of the most obviously fabulistic of London's fiction, his dog stories, was their problematical accuracy in depicting the conditions of natural life. After the great success of *The Call of the Wild* and *White Fang* (as well as the contemporary popularity of other nature fiction), Theodore Roosevelt, in a famous controversy of 1907, attacked London (among others) as a "nature faker." Referring to the fight between a lynx and a wolf in *White Fang*, Roosevelt commented, "Nobody who really knew anything about either a lynx or a wolf would write such nonsense." He then went on to reveal his misunderstanding of the form in which London was writing. "If the stories of these writers were written in the spirit that inspired Mowgli [the human figure in Kipling's *The Jungle Book*], . . . we should be content to read, enjoy, and accept them as fables. . . . But when such fables are written by a make-believe realist, the matter assumes an entirely different complexion."[2]

Of course, criticism of London has advanced far beyond Roosevelt's demand that animal fiction should announce itself clearly as either fabulistic or realistic. For example, in a striking reading of *The Call of the Wild* and *White Fang*, [critic] Earle Labor has suggested that the permanent appeal of these works is that they are beast fables whose endorsement of the myth of the hero and of the value of primordial strength rings true in our collective unconscious.[3] Labor's Jungian [after Swiss psychiatrist Carl Jung] reading of these works is the most useful which has yet appeared, but I believe that a more immediate reason for the appeal and holding power of London's best work lies in their form.

London's work falls roughly into three groups related to his "natural" inclination to work in the fable/parable form. The first, which includes *The Call of the Wild* and *White Fang* as well as such stories as "To Build a Fire" and "The Chinago," reveals his ability to rely unconsciously yet with great success on the underlying characteristics of the fable/parable. The second, which includes *The Iron Heel* and such stories as "The Apostate" and "The Strength of the Strong," suggests that when London wrote consciously in the parable form—as he did in these works—he sacrificed power for ideological obviousness. And the third, which includes a large number of London's novels and short stories, but most significantly *The Sea-Wolf*, indicates that London's efforts to write conventional fiction were usually handicapped by his inadequacies in this form, but that such works are occasionally rescued by their fabulistic element. Finally, I will also suggest that much that is distinctive and valuable in London's autobiographical writing—in *The Road, Martin Eden*, and *John Barleycorn*—can be viewed as an extension into this form of his penchant for the fable/parable.

The Call of the Wild and *White Fang* are companion allegories [symbolic stories] of the response of human nature to heredity and environment. Both Buck and White Fang begin their lives with a mixture of the primitive and the civilized in their condition. Buck is raised in the southland (London's allegorical setting for civilization), but, like all dogs, has an atavistic strain of wolf in his makeup. White Fang, though largely wolf and though bred in the far north, contains an element of the civilized through his part-dog mother. The novels demonstrate the effects of a change in environment on the two dogs. Buck, abducted into a northland world of the ruthless struggle for existence, calls forth from his racial past the strength and cunning necessary to survive in this world, and eventually becomes the leader of a wolf pack in a people-less wilderness. White Fang is drawn into civilization, first by Indians, then by miners, and finally, in the southland, by upper-middle-class ranchers, and becomes doglike in his loyalty and love toward his master.

What appeals in the two works is not London's dramatization of a particular late nineteenth-century Darwinian [after English naturalist Charles Darwin] formulation but rather his powerful use of the principal ethical thrust and formal characteristics of the fable, with an admixture as well of the parable. Characterization is at a minimum in the two works; dogs and men are types and the types themselves are moral in nature. In *Call*, Charles, Hal, and Mercedes (the three "tenderfoot" Klondikers who buy Buck) are Vanity and Ignorance, and John Thornton is Loyalty and Love. The dogs in the story are even more clearly moral types—Laziness, Envy, Fear, Honesty, and so on. In *White Fang*, Kiche is the Mother, Beauty Smith (who exhibits White Fang) is Evil, and Weedon Scott is Thornton's counterpart. Setting is allegorical in both works, with London exaggerating for symbolic clarity both the "softness" of the south and the competitive animality of the north. And action is symbolic within the clear lines of thematic movement of Buck's return to the primitive and White Fang's engagement by civilization. Perhaps most important of all, theme itself is essentially proverbial rather than ideological. It is not so much Darwin and [English philosopher Herbert] Spencer who supply the thematic core of the two novels as Aesop and the Bible. For *Call of the Wild* proposes the wisdom of the beast fable that the strong, the shrewd, and the cunning shall prevail when, as is progressively true in this story, life is bestial. And *White Fang* endorses the Christian wisdom that all shall lie down together in peace when love predominates.

Both *Call* and *White Fang* contain—to a degree not usually sufficiently stressed—a strong element of the Christian parable within their beast fable emphasis on the competitive nature of experience. Buck's response to the kindness, justness, and warmth of Thornton is love; it is only with the death of Thornton that he becomes the Ghost Dog of the wilderness. And White Fang, when rescued from the brutality of Beauty Smith by Weedon Scott and when "educated" in affection by Scott, also responds with love. The moral allegory is clear in both works. Man hovers between the primitive and the civilized both in his makeup and in his world, and it is his capacity for love which often determines which direction he will take. Again, this theme is not so much specifically ideological as it is racial wisdom, with that wisdom embodied in a form which makes it pleasingly evident.

An obvious question, given the similarities in theme and form between the two works, is why *The Call of the Wild* is generally held to be superior to *White Fang*. An answer lies, I believe, in the greater conformity of *Call* to the beast fable form in two significant areas. First, *White Fang* makes greater pretentions to the range and fullness of a novel. Fabulistic brevity and conciseness, and thus symbolic sharpness, are sacrificed for lengthy development of each phase of White Fang's career. And since we can anticipate from the beginning the nature and direction of his evolution, the doldrums occasionally set in. But also, as Earle Labor has pointed out, we are inherently more interested in an account of a return to the primitive than one of an advance into civilization. Labor suggests, as I noted earlier, that this difference in attraction lies in the greater appeal which *Call* makes to our unconscious longing for primitive simplicity and freedom. But this greater holding power may derive as well—and more immediately— from the fuller endorsement in *Call* of the Aesopian wisdom that the strong prevail. There is not much love in Aesop, but there is much demonstration that it is better to be powerful in a world in which power controls destiny.

Notes

1. I have been aided in my understanding of the fable by Marcel Gutwirth's published Mellon lecture, *Fable* (New Orleans: Graduate School of Tulane Univ., Fall, 1980), and by B.E. Perry's "Fable," *Studium Generale*, 12 (1959): 17–37.

2. Theodore Roosevelt, "Men Who Misinterpret Nature," in *The Works of Theodore Roosevelt* (New York: Scribner, 1926), V, 368-69; reprinted from *Everybody's Magazine*, 16 (June 1907): 770-74.

3. Earle Labor, "Jack London's *Mondo Cane: The Call of the Wild* and *White Fang*," *Jack London Newsletter*, 1 (July-Dec. 1967): 2-13; reprinted in Labor's *Jack London* (New York: Twayne, 1974) pp. 69-81.

The Call of the Wild Pits Society Against Wildness

Charles N. Watson Jr.

Charles N. Watson Jr. taught at Syracuse University. He is the editor of The Son of the Wolf: Tales of the Far North *and has published articles on American authors including Robert Frost and Herman Melville.*

In the following viewpoint, Watson compares The Call of the Wild *to two other great American novels,* The Adventures of Huckleberry Finn *and* Moby-Dick. *In his quest to escape from society, Buck resembles Huck Finn, who similarly wishes to light out for the territory at the end of his story. As in* The Adventures of Huckleberry Finn, The Call of the Wild *presents two conflicting alternatives Buck must choose between: civilization and the wild. As in* Moby-Dick, The Call of the Wild *dramatizes wildness in terms of whiteness. Like the eponymous white whale of Melville's novel, Buck too disappears into a vast expanse of nature to ultimately become a mythical beast.*

*T*he Call of the Wild can no more be dismissed as a dog story than *Moby-Dick* can be dismissed as a whale story. Indeed, [critic] Alfred Kazin's fine insight—that [American novelist Herman] Melville's Ishmael "sees the whale's view of things," that he speaks for the primordial, trans-human world of natures—can equally well be applied to [author Jack] London. Both Melville and London attain a kind of double vision, sensing the alien character of the natural world while at the same time feeling a deep kinship with it. This is not a matter of observing, as some critics have done, that the dog story in-

Charles N. Watson Jr., *The Novels of Jack London: A Reappraisal*. Madison: University of Wisconsin Press, 1983, pp. 33–52. Copyright © 1983 University of Wisconsin Press. All rights reserved. Reproduced by permission.

volves a human "allegory," a term implying that Buck is merely a human being disguised as a dog. Rather, the intuition at the heart of the novel is that the processes of individuation in a dog, a wolf, or a human child are not fundamentally different. Somehow, out of the dim memories of his own childhood, London recaptures the groping steps by which the very young deal with the mystifying sensations of their world, learning that snow is cold and fluffy, that fire burns, that some people are kind and others cruel. This is the "primordial vision" that [critic] Earle Labor has rightly insisted is a distinctive facet of London's imagination.

Society vs. the Wilderness

But *The Call of the Wild* is about society as well as about the wilderness—or rather, like [London's earlier novel] *A Daughter of the Snows*, it is about the conflict between the two, a conflict that reaches its height in the final chapter, when Buck finds himself unable to choose between the civilizing influence of John Thornton and the increasingly insistent call of his primitive brothers. The conflict is resolved when Thornton dies and Buck leaves civilized life for good, but that departure is only the culmination of a movement toward the wild that has been taking place throughout the book. The movement is not steady; sometimes Buck will advance one step toward the wild only to be cast back again toward civilization. Still, the fundamental movement is clear, and it can be regarded from two seemingly opposite perspectives. Approached from the assumptions of Zolaesque [after French novelist Émile Zola] naturalism, it will seem atavistic—a reversion to savagery, a process of degeneration. On the other hand, from the standpoint of romantic primitivism, it will appear to embody the forward movement of an initiation rite, through which Buck attains maturity and even apotheosis as a mythic hero.

Both of these views accurately describe the action of the novel. Indeed, London himself reveals the same ambivalence when he says of Buck: "His development (or retrogression) was rapid." This "divided stream" of American naturalism was first recognized by [critic] Charles Child Walcutt, who saw the materialistic thrust of the new naturalism at odds with the strains of transcendental idealism and romantic individualism that continued to exert a strong influence on American fiction. [American novelist] Frank Norris and Jack London offer particularly good examples of this uneasy combination. Norris, in fact, devoted several of his critical essays to promoting the idea that Zola and other naturalists, including himself, were actually romanticists. The result for all of these novelists is a fruitful tension between the naturalistic impulse, with its emphasis on society and environment, and the romantic impulse, which emphasizes the power of the exceptional individual to act on his own. Such a tension, as so many critics have observed, is one of the most fundamental themes of American fiction.

The Call of the Wild and *The Adventures of Huckleberry Finn*

This indigenous American quality can be seen more clearly if one observes the structural parallels between *The Call of the Wild* and *The Adventures of Huckleberry Finn*. As the two novels begin, each young protagonist lives in society under the protection of a benevolent foster parent. Each undertakes a journey away from that sheltered world, encountering in his travels several varieties of civilized virtue and folly. Intermittently, however, he feels the counterinfluence of the natural world and the anarchic impulse toward escape; and when each at the end is nearly adopted by another benevolent foster parent, he instead heeds the call of the wild and lights out for the territory.

Despite manifest differences of tone and narrative method—*The Call*, for example, lacks the satirical, picaresque qualities of Twain's novel—these structural and thematic parallels suggest that both *Huckleberry Finn* and *The Call* are sustained at least in part by a common vision. What they share is the perennial American dream of escape and freedom associated with the natural world. As critics of *Huckleberry Finn* have repeatedly recognized, it is the river itself, and the life Huck and Jim lead there, that holds the strongest fascination for the reader. In this idyllic world, the stirrings of primitive life reassert themselves when the two fugitives, rejecting the desiccated piety of civilization, reinvent a natural mythology as they speculate about the origin of the stars, wondering "whether they was made, or only just happened." Jim suggests that "the moon could a *laid* them," and Huck allows that "that looked kind of reasonable . . . because I've seen a frog lay most as many, so of course it could be done." Just as Huck begins to reexperience the world mythopoetically, from the ground up and from the sky down, London's Buck must discover, in himself and in the wilderness, the primordial sensations that lead him to reject the conventions of civilized life. Hence it is no disparagement to say that both of these are "escape novels," for the impulse toward escape—toward the world of wish and dream—exists in all of us, and one of the functions of fiction is to fulfill it. There is, no doubt, a higher function that fiction can serve: to take us not merely away from our daily realities but into a reality we have not yet experienced or have experienced only imperfectly. The best "escape fiction"—including *Huckleberry Finn* and *The Call of the Wild*—serves that purpose, too.

Buck as a Work Dog

During the long middle section of the novel, Buck is at the mercy of his owners, and the structure of episodes is governed chiefly by the contrast between two Klondike types, the hardened sourdough and the ignorant *chechaquo* [newcomer]. Francois and Perrault, with their rough but humane discipline and their hardy devotion to work, contrast sharply with the hapless incapables: the mindlessly vicious Hal and Charles, who club the dogs for failing to perform impossible tasks, and the self-indulgent, sentimental Mercedes, who protests the whipping of the "poor dears" even while insisting that the bone-weary dogs pull her own weight on the already over-loaded sled. This trio, in turn, contrasts sharply with Buck's final master, the kindly John Thornton.

But these episodes offer more than a gallery of Klondike types. They also serve to establish the civilized values against which the wilderness must compete, for human society in this novel is not an irredeemable disaster. Indeed, its most attractive virtues serve as a necessary counterweight to the ever more insistent call of the wild. Of central though qualified value is the pride of work, and even more deeply attractive is the value of love. For Buck, both love and work fulfill a profound need, though neither can finally compete with the deepest need of all—the one ecstatically fulfilled in the blood ritual of the hunt.

In his early years on Judge Miller's estate, though no "mere pampered house-dog," Buck resembles [London's character] Vance Corliss of *A Daughter of the Snows*, living the easy life of a "sated aristocrat," developing his muscles not through work but through play. The abrupt transition to the northland introduces him to the world of labor. "No lazy, sun-kissed life was this," he finds, "with nothing to do but loaf and be bored." Instead he must perform the tasks that in the southland were assigned to draft-horses. Yet once he has absorbed this blow to his dignity, he discovers that "though the work was hard . . . he did not particularly despise it." Gradually accommodating himself to the harness, he experiences the "nameless, incomprehensible pride of the trail and trace—that pride which holds does in the toil to the last gasp." As it does for [English novelist Joseph] Conrad's [protagonist] Marlow in *Heart of Darkness*, work constitutes a source of order in the midst of primitive chaos.

An Alternative to Work

Nevertheless, Buck's attitude toward work grows increasingly ambivalent. Part of the reason lies in the nature of the work itself, especially in the cautionary example of two other dogs of the team, Dave and Sol-leks, who seem the very incarnation of passionate devotion to toil. Otherwise uninspired and phlegmatic, they are "utterly transformed by the harness." The labor of the trail seemed "the supreme expression of their being." Under the inspiriting mastership of Francois and Perrault, such devotion seems admirable, almost heroic; but after the team passes into the hands of the "Scotch half-breed," the work gets harder, more routine, and less rewarding. Though Buck continues to take pride in it "after the manner of Dave and Sol-leks," he no longer enjoys it, for it is "a monotonous life, operating with machine-like regularity." The "pride of trail and trace" has become the drudgery of the work-beast—a fate dramatized when Dave wears down in the traces and must be shot. Thereafter the ineptitude of Hal, Charles, and Mercedes reduces what is left of the nobility of labor to meaningless, grinding, and ultimately fatal toil.

The decreasing attractions of the work itself are accentuated by the ever more alluring alternative of the wild. The conflict heightens when the team first reaches Dawson, where in the civilized daylight world it seems "the ordained order of things that dogs should work." But though by day these dogs haul cabin logs and firewood and freight, most of them are of the "wild wolf husky breed" in whose "nocturnal song, a weird and eerie chant," it is "Buck's delight to join." On the trail, as well, though the work is "a delight to him," it becomes "a greater delight slyly to precipitate a fight amongst his mates and tangle the traces." This act is more than a momentary imp of the perverse; there is method in it. What Buck seeks as an alternative to order and work is the deeper satisfaction of the irrational, the anarchic, and the demonic, symbolized by the hunt and the kill. Challenging the leadership of Spitz by plunging the team into disorder, he hopes to precipitate the climactic fight that will confirm his devotion to the primordial life.

The trail and the mining camp thus provide halfway stations between the extremes of civilization and savagery, calling forth the values of hardihood, discipline, and devotion. The other civilized value—the value of love—is also associated with contrasting landscapes. The loving kindness that Buck experiences with Judge Miller and John Thornton is associated with the southland, and with its central images: fire, sun, daylight, summer, and warmth. The antithesis of this world of love is, of course, the northland wilderness, whose images are darkness, frost, moonlight, winter, and cold. London weaves these images into the texture of the novel, subtly establishing the natural rhythms of Buck's divided life.

Like work, love is a source of order—not the order of disciplined movement but that of the stability and security of an enclosed space. Its locale is not the trail but the fireside or the sunlit clearing. In the beginning, Buck basks securely on Judge Miller's estate in the "sun-kissed" Santa Clara Valley, and "on wintry nights he lay at the Judge's feet before the roaring library fire." The secluded domesticity of the house, "back from the road, half hidden among the trees," as well as the "rows of vine-clad servants' cottages, an endless and orderly array of outhouses, long grape arbors, green pastures, orchards, and berry patches," make the estate an oasis of pastoral serenity, just as the fire in the library suggests an island of civilization in the midst of a wintry darkness.

But though temporarily under the protection of a benevolent owner and the maternal warmth of the southland, Buck will soon be abducted into a life of wandering orphanhood in the north. A measure of his loss, of his need for an enfolding maternal presence, arises during his first night on the trail when he searches for a warm place to sleep. Seeing the light and warm glow in the tent of Francois and Perrault, he seeks refuge there but is driven back violently into the cold, where, "miserable and disconsolate, he wandered about among the many tents, only to find that one place was as cold as another." At last he learns the trick of burrowing under the snow, discovering paradoxically that the only warmth lies there.

Afterwards, under the firm discipline of the two Frenchmen, his movement toward self-sufficiency is rapid. But the extraordinary kindness of John Thornton soon causes him to regress to the dependency and idealistic devotion of childhood and consequently to experience the foster-child's fear of abandonment: "For a long time after his rescue, Buck did not like Thornton to get out of his sight. From the moment he left the tent to when he entered it again, Buck would follow at his heels. His transient masters since he had come into the Northland had bred in him a fear that no master could be permanent. He was afraid that Thornton would pass out of his life as Perrault and Francois and the Scotch half-breed had passed out. Even in the night, in his dreams, he was haunted by this fear."

Yet this regression is temporary. By the time Thornton is killed, Buck has completed his rite of passage into adulthood, and his grief, though deep and genuine, is but the last of his civilized emotions, his farewell to his life as a son. Not even this deeply affectionate relationship can entirely heal the division in Buck's nature, for in spite of its "soft civilizing influence" on him, "the strain of the primitive . . . remained alive and active. Faithfulness and devotion, things born of fire and roof, were his; yet he retained his wildness and wiliness. He was a thing of the wild, come in from the wild to sit by John Thornton's fire, rather than a dog of the soft Southland stamped with the marks of generations of civilization." . . .

London weaves one further strand: the evocative Melvillean [after American novelist Herman Melville] symbol of whiteness. This symbol, in fact, is a recurrent one in London's

"It was to the death."

Buck and Spitz fight to the death in The Call of the Wild. © Susan Isakson/Alamy.

writing. It appears in the early story "The White Silence," where the title signals "the ghostly wastes of a dead world," convincing man of his insignificance. It recurs in the eerie terror of the "white death" that Smoke Bellew and Labiskwee encounter during their flight through the mountains in "Wonder of Woman"—a "weird mist" with the "stinging thickness of cold fire." And finally, as the White Logic, it becomes the central image of [London's autobiographical work] *John Barleycorn*, where it implies the ultimate reality, the coldly terrifying truth to be found beyond all comforting illusions. In *The Call of the Wild*, it is not only the menace of the frozen landscape; it is also the personification of that landscape in a white beast, whom Buck must hunt, defeat, and displace—whom he must, in a sense, become.

Buck's first crucial rite of passage occurs in the stirring conflict with Spitz. As the lead dog doomed to be deposed by a younger, stronger rival, Spitz is the symbolic father, the incarnation of the demonic white wilderness of Buck's ancestors. Their climactic encounter, with its atmosphere of ghostly whiteness and its impression of ritualistic compulsions, seems an instinctive reenactment of an episode that has taken place since the beginnings of animal life. The fight is preceded and foreshadowed by a ritualistic hunt for a white rabbit, during which Buck and Spitz compete for the honor of the kill. In the "wan white moonlight" the rabbit flashes across the snow "like some pale frost wraith," while Buck, leading the pack and scenting the kill, anticipates the baptismal moment when he will "wash his muzzle to the eyes in warm blood." . . .

[London's] knowledge of [Herman] Melville's *Moby-Dick* (1851) could have suggested to him a . . . cluster of images and rituals centering on the demonic associations of whiteness.

The Call of the Wild *and* Moby-Dick

Melville's narrative of the hunt for the fabled white whale must have been on London's mind during the writing of *The Call of the Wild*, as it certainly was a few months later when he wrote *The Sea-Wolf*. He may have recalled, for example, the scene in "The Quarter-Deck" when Captain Ahab and his harpooners swear a diabolic oath to hunt Moby-Dick to his death. As the rest of the crew "formed a circle round the group," their "wild eyes met his, as the bloodshot eyes of the prairie wolves meet the eye of their leader, ere he rushes on at their head in the trail of the bison." Just as Melville based his romance in part on a legendary sperm whale, London may have known of a "ghost dog" story then current in Alaskan folklore. Without question, he knew Melville's chapter "The Whiteness of the Whale," in which several images of demonic whiteness are drawn from landscapes of snow. Conjuring up the "eternal frosted desolateness" of snowcapped mountains, Ishmael imagines "what a fearfulness it would be to lose oneself in such inhuman solitudes." Later, he associates the "dumb blankness, full of meaning, in a wide landscape of snows" with the "colorless, all-color of atheism from which we shrink." These images, which Earle Labor has compared to London's description of the ominous landscape in "The White Silence," are equally pertinent to *The Call of the Wild*, in which the hunt for the white rabbit is climaxed by the death struggle with the white dog.

London would have been especially alert to Melville's instances of fabulous white beasts of the American wilderness, whose qualities anticipate those of Spitz and, later, of Buck himself. Most notable is Melville's observation that "to the noble Iroquois, the midwinter sacrifice of the sacred White Dog was by far the holiest festival of their theology, that spotless, faithful creature being held the purest envoy they could send to the Great Spirit with the annual tidings of their own fidelity." It is precisely such a ritual sacrifice of the totem animal that [Austrian neurologist Sigmund] Freud saw as a symbolic reenactment of the primal crime of patricide, which is so strongly implied in Buck's killing of Spitz.

Into the White Wilderness

The final phase of the initiation into the white wilderness occurs when Buck accompanies Thornton in the search for the "fabled lost mine" of the east. . . .

There remains only for Buck to pass into Indian legend as the "Ghost Dog that runs at the head of the pack." If London remembered a northland legend of a ghost dog, he may also have recalled Melville's description of the White Steed of the Prairies, "with the dignity of a thousand monarchs in his lofty, overscorning carriage":

> He was the elected Xerxes of vast herds of wild horses, whose pastures in those days were only fenced by the Rocky Mountains and the Alleghanies. . . . A most imperial and archangelical apparition of that unfallen, western world, which to the eyes of the old trappers and hunters revived the glories of those primeval times when Adam walked majestic as a god, bluff-bowed and fearless as this mighty steed . . . always to the bravest Indians he was the object of trembling reverence and awe. Nor can it be questioned from what stands on legendary record of this noble horse, that it was his spiritual whiteness chiefly, which so clothed him with divineness; and that this divineness had that in it which, though commanding worship, at the same time enforced a certain nameless terror.

In his combination of divinity and demonism, his "spiritual whiteness" evoking both "reverence" and "terror," the White Steed becomes the incarnation of the primeval wilderness precisely as Buck becomes to the Indians both a sign of the "Evil Spirit" and yet, as the Ghost Dog, the object of a kind of spiritual awe. His ascendancy as father and leader is signaled by the "change in the breed of timber wolves," some now being seen with a "rift of white centring down the chest." As the great white whale triumphantly swims away from the sinking *Pequod* [the whaling ship in *Moby-Dick*], so does Buck elude the desperate Yeehats, "running at the head of the pack through the pale moonlight or glimmering borealis, leaping gigantic above his fellows." His apotheosis [elevation to god-like stature] as the Ghost Dog of the north is complete.

London's Animal Depictions Are Deceptive

John Perry

John Perry is the author of James A. Herne: The American Ibsen *and editor of the Jack London short story collection* Thirteen Tales of Horror.

In the following viewpoint, Perry writes that Jack London's depiction of nature was more fictional than factual. London was caught up in the prevailing philosophy of European literary naturalism, which held that human behavior is driven by essential needs just as is animal behavior. London's animal characters, Perry argues, are men in fur, and their behavior in his fiction is more barbaric and primitive than in real life. Wolves, for example, are usually more fearful of men than vice versa, yet London was so caught up in the myth of the ferocious, ruthless wolf that he concocted a false picture of these animals.

[A uthor Jack] London's absorption with nature's "dominant primordial beasts," his work roving between the worlds of romance and raw primitivism, borders on the ridiculous, the kind of thing H.L. Mencken called "muck for the multitudes." This even mars *The Call of the Wild,* in which Buck dreams about a caveman sitting around an ancient fire, sometimes scurrying up trees for protection from wild beasts. "The hair of this man was long and matted, and his head slanted back under it from the eyes. He uttered strange sounds, and seemed very much afraid of the darkness, into which he peered continually, clutching in his hand, which hung midway between knee and foot, a stick with a heavy stone made fast to the end. He was all but naked, a ragged and fire-scorched skin hanging part way down his back, but on his body there was much hair." . . .

Exalting the Primitive

After London's remarks in "Revolution" that cavemen loafed, generally ate well, and breathed fresh air, their children enjoying the good life, critics raved, the *Berkeley Advance* roasting his idea that "the man who crawled in and out of a hole in the hill was better fed than millions of people today." The *San Francisco Chronicle* jeered:

> Jack London declares that the cave dweller was much better off than the laboring man of today. He thinks that the mental and material welfare of the latter would be improved by reverting to the anarchism which prevailed in the days of the cave dwellers, and insists that there are today seven million people in the world enrolled with the sworn purpose of overthrowing society. If there are so many avowed enemies of society as London declares, they ought to be able to form a big enough colony in some part of the world to furnish a practical demonstration of the beauties of their ism. The chances are if such a colony should ever be formed it would not be in existence long before society would have to step in to prevent its members cutting each other's throats.

Why London's interest in cavedom? It certainly didn't embrace the period's "return to nature" talk, an American pipe dream since the time of [Henry David] Thoreau. Perhaps the *Bookman* explained: "It is the animal side of human nature that Mr. London always delights in exalting, in all the relations of life." In such a woeful world, man's fighting instinct dominates, so does human depravity. Ethics become absurd, man's assurance of broken bones and starving stomachs. Primitivism also negates the spine of [English writer and philosopher] Herbert Spencer's credo that humanity evolves, not devolves. Regression, of course, spells out decay, another central London theme, from Alaska's white wilderness to the decayed tropical vegetation of South Sea islands—a peculiar slant during America's strenuous age of Rooseveltian [after President Theodore Roosevelt] virility and optimism.

Preoccupation with European Naturalism

The period's literary preoccupation with European naturalism, which often reduced men to wild, elemental beasts, provided a popular framework for London's primitivism, which [critic] Frederick J. Hoffman calls "an interesting sideshow in the naturalistic carnival." London compared one of the mob's hands in *The Iron Heel* to claws and hoofs. A Goat-Man and Fish-Man play roles in *A Son of the Sun*. Humphrey Van Weyden and Maud Brewster revive "like bugs and crawling things" on their deserted island. The narrator of "Li Wan, the Fair" comments: "And over all, like a monstrous race of ants, was flung an army of men—mud-covered, dirty, dishevelled men, who crawled in and out of the holes of their digging, crept like big bugs along the flumes." In "The End of the Story," a rabbit bone is grafted to a man's arm, creating the perfect limb. And in *The People of the Abyss*, London compares the submerged tenth to wolves and other animals of prey, calling one boy "a young cub seeking his food in the jungle of empire, preying upon the weak and being preyed upon by the strong."

Such remarks support London's view, one stated in such articles as "The Somnambulists" that beneath the skin, man and beast share common inheritances. Remove civilized man to a remote region? He's soon reduced to an elemental force, devoid of values, stalking food to survive. "Morals are not the important thing, nor enlightenment—nor civilization," said [American writer] Mark Twain. "A man can do absolutely well without them, but he can't do without *something to eat*. The supremest thing is the needs of the body, not of the mind &

spirit." London illustrates this in [his short story] "Bâtard." It also happens to the peaceful Buck in *The Call of the Wild*. Man even resembles the beasts, assuming their physical features, their instinctual behavior. "What with the Fear of the North, the mental strain, and the ravages of the disease," wrote London in "In a Far Country," "they lost all semblance of humanity, taking on the appearance of wild beasts, hunted and desperate." Both Buck and White Fang are men dressed in furs. When they brutally maim and devour opponents, London means humans, releasing complex hostilities in his makeup against the world, hostilities again traced to his birth and feelings of inferiority. Even Macmillan Company admitted this in *Jack London: His Life and Literary Works*: "In his two most important books, *The Call of the Wild*, and *White Fang*, he has reduced thought and emotion to their lowest terms. He has dared to treat animals like human beings—not symbolically, be it noted, but realistically and naturally—because he recognizes no essential difference between the so-called lower animals and man." . . .

London Misinforming Readers

London . . . misinformed readers about animal behavior in *The Call of the Wild*. Buck, returning to the spoils of a kill, finds a dozen wolverines, among nature's most vicious creatures. "He scattered them like chaff; and those that fled left two behind who would quarrel no more." (London used *wolves* and *wolverines* interchangeably in his stories, not realizing that vicious wolverines would have slaughtered White Fang.) Buck also beats an entire wolf pack. In the 1918 posthumous *Michael, Brother of Jerry*, Michael, a fox terrier puppy, breaks the back of a gigantic Persian cat, its tail the size of a muscle man's arm, then takes on two full-grown fox terriers, crushing the foot of one and nearly severing the other's jugular vein. He even leaves the ship's captain bleeding on deck. As Theodore Roosevelt reasoned: "The modern 'nature faker' is of course an object of derision to every scientist worthy of the name, to every real lover of the wilderness, to every faunal naturalist, to every true hunter or nature lover. But it is evident that he completely deceives many good people who are wholly ignorant of wild life. Sometimes he draws on his own imagination for his fictions; sometimes he gets them second-hand from irresponsible guides or trappers or Indians."

The wolf remains Jack London's most outrageous deception, an animal he associated with cunning, fierce strength, and legendary inheritance traced to Romulus and Remus. "In spite of our sober biological outlook," writes [American author] Barry Lopez, "we can't seem to escape our fear of . . . [the wolf] hunter, any more than we can deny a fondness for the . . . [animal] because he seems to represent valued things that are slipping away from us—courage, wildness, self-sufficiency. Our fascination with the wolf may be rooted in a perception of him as the symbol of an internal war, the conflict between rational and instinctual behavior. This is the wolf of Aesopian fable." Lopez adds in *Of Wolves and Men* that "London's novels show a preoccupation with 'the brute nature' in men, which he symbolized in the wolf. . . . But it is, ultimately, a neurotic fixation with machismo that has as little to do with wolves as the drinking, whoring, and fighting side of man's brute nature."

In London stories, wolves track adventurers across Klondike trails, sniffing blood stains on the virgin snow, devouring them alive. In "The Story of Jees Uck," Neil Bonner brings a brute into his post, "but the beast, mere domesticated wolf that it was, rebelled, and sought out dark corners and snarled and bit him in the leg, and was finally beaten and driven forth." Old Koskoosh, of course, is eaten alive by wolves in "The Law of Life." "He saw the flashing forms of gray, the gleaming eyes, the lolling tongues, and slavered fangs. . . . A cold muzzle thrust against his cheek. . . . He waved his brand wildly, and sniffs turned to snarls; but the panting brutes refused to scatter. Now one wormed his chest forward, dragging his haunches after, now a second, now a third; but never a one drew back." In "Love of Life," a sick man and sick wolf try to outwit each other, the man finally strangling the anemic beast, sucking blood from its throat. London spent an entire chapter in *White Fang* on wolves: After eating Henry's partner, the pack chases Henry across the white wilderness, snarling and salivating, leaping at limbs and throat in camp. A fire frightens them until help miraculously arrives at dawn.

The Truth About Wolves

Millions of Americans swallowed London's cruel fantasies as truth, not realizing human beings terrify wolves. "In North America, no scientifically acceptable evidence is available to support the claim that healthy wild wolves are dangerous to man," writes L. David Mech in *The Wolf*. "Even stronger evidence that healthy North American wolves are harmless to humans can be found in the many well-documented accounts of various researchers who have worked in wolf country. . . . In my own experiences with wolves I have never come close to danger."

[Canadian author] Farley Mowat tells this story in *Never Cry Wolf*: "Quite by accident I had pitched my tent within ten yards of one of the major paths used by the wolves when they were going to, or coming from, their hunting grounds to the westward; and only a few hours after I had taken up residence one of the wolves came back from a trip and discovered me and my tent. . . . It was true that I wanted to be inconspicuous, but I felt uncomfortable at being so totally ignored. Nevertheless, during the two weeks which followed, one or more wolves used the track past my tent almost every night—and never, except on one memorable occasion, did they evince the slightest interest in me."

Naturalist cinematographer Bill Mason, who filmed *Cry of the Wild* for the Canadian Wildlife Service, writes me: "My captive wolves were terrified of me, despite all my efforts to befriend them. Only pups taken from the mother before two weeks old could be tamed and raised to accept the presence of humans without fear. If there is one single thing that I learned from all my experiences with wolves, it's that I would stake unequivocally that wolves are terrified of people. In fact I staked my life on it by travelling unarmed among them and alone. The only dangers I faced were from the extreme cold."

Perhaps Roger A. Caras (author of *The Custer Wolf*, ABC-TV news correspondent and former vice president of the Humane Society of the United States) makes the most penetrating remark about London and wolves, writing me that London was "an incurable romantic whose truth was instantly made and served up as needed. . . . He was not an authority on wolves, dogs, people, places or truth. He wrote and they bought it so he wrote some more." Caras comments about London's Yukon stories: "He certainly was also devoted to the macho image. I have been around sled dogs (I cared for a championship team) and I have been in the Arctic and in Eskimo villages. It is rather more peaceful than super jock Jack London portrays."

London's Obsession with Wolves

An obsession with wolves haunted London's life, another expression of his pathological involvement with symbols of fear and violence. As Sidney Alexander says, "The trouble with Jack London was that he wasn't sure whether he was a man or a wolf." London used the name in the title of two books: *The Sea-Wolf* and *The Son of the Wolf*, dedicating *The God of His Fathers* "to the daughters of the wolf who have bred and suckled a race of men." He also wrote a short story called "Brown Wolf," a pet husky's name. *White Fang* is called "The Fighting Wolf." Burning Daylight sleeps beneath wolf skins. Other characters wear wolf skin caps. Thomas Regan in *Hearts of Three* is called "The Wolf of Wall Street." London had a wolf's head on his engraved stationery and bookmarks, signed his letters "Wolf," and named his sprawling ranch at Glen Ellen "Wolf House." George Sterling called him "Wolf,"—something he asked [his second wife] Charmian to do more often. "In all his writings Jack London is changing dogs into wolves and wolves into dogs," remarked Stephen Graham. "In the course of it all London himself became a civilized dog, reconciled to kennel and master. But he constantly bays at men and the moon to assure them that he is wolf at heart."

London's Essay "Husky: The Wolf-Dog of the North" Offers Insights into His Dog Novels

S.K. Robisch

S.K. Robisch has taught American literature and American studies at Purdue University. He now works as an independent scholar.

In his study of wolves in American myth and literature, Robisch discusses London's early essay "Husky: The Wolf-Dog of the North," written when the author's Yukon experiences were fresh in his memory. In this essay, London describes the characteristics of the dogs that would figure so prominently in his life and in his writing. While London intended The Call of the Wild *and* White Fang *to be paired novels, Robisch suggests that a third work, the short story "Bâtard," must be considered to complicate London's notion of the wolf-dog. Robisch examines nature versus nurture in London's three great dog stories, finding* Call *to be a version of the good dog,* White Fang *the naturally evil, and "Bâtard" constructed evil. Robisch contends that the depiction of Buck leading the pack is entirely false as a wolf pack would not accept a husky into its fold. Ultimately* The Call of the Wild *is merely a dog story, and it is in* White Fang *that London takes his dog stories to a "telling conclusion."*

Perhaps the most important short piece that London wrote giving us insight to the creation of the Great Dog novels is the essay "Husky: The Wolf-Dog of the North," published in *Harper's* in June of 1900. [F]or London "wolf-dog" signifies the husky breed, what would then have been called inter-

S.K. Robisch, *Wolves and the Wolf Myth in American Literature*. Reno: University of Nevada Press, 2009, pp. 300–307. Copyright © 2009 by University of Nevada Press. Reprinted with permission of the University of the Nevada Press.

changeably the Alaskan or Siberian husky. London's idea, and a correct one, behind this phrase was that husky was closer to its lupine [wolflike] morphology than most other dogs—an opportunity to examine atavism [reversion to an earlier form] that would not be lost on him. Men don't keep wolves in London's works; they keep huskies and the occasional hybrid. The wolf is the denizen of wilderness, motivated entirely by the nature that is alive in (but only partly driving) the wolf-dog. In his description of the husky London does reveal an essentialism that still pervades the language of the breed-obsessed. The breed, rather than the individual, determines thought and action: "They are far from humble, as their wild ancestry attests. They may be beaten into submission, but that will not prevent them still snarling their hatred. They may be starved into apparent docility, and then die, suddenly, with teeth fast locked in a brother's throat, torn to pieces by their comrades." This first tenet of the breed is itself an unintended ironic comment on the nature of the human being instead. It's difficult to tell here whether London's comment is a declaration about the breed or a declaration about the perception of cruel and ignorant human beings trying to train huskies by torturing them. It seems, unfortunately, that he is of the former disposition. He writes, "Rather, has little attention been accorded them because the interest of man has gravitated inexorably toward the natural, mineral, and social features of that far-northerly land." Huskies are possessions, tools, commodities, features of the civilizing impulse. This tells us something about the narrator's (if not the author's) relationship to his focalizers in the novels.

His next tenets of the breed include the following:

1. "No white man" ever figured out how to tie up a husky, but the Indians learned to tie with a stick through the collar to keep them from chewing the thong. The rope is then staked to the ground at the other end. The husky's close connection

to its wolf origin is indicated here, wolves being notorious es-capees and runners when kept as pets.

2. "In the summer-time . . . the huskies are thrown on their own resources." That is, when the winter work is through and the sleds are no longer running, the wolf-dogs are left to go feral. The assumption is that this toughens them and drives them back into their primal selves, to reestablish order as (it is generalized) a wolf pack would.

3. "They are superb travelers . . . making runs of seventy or eighty miles." This would be the most lupine of their char-acteristics, but not in London's preferred universe.

4. "It is in fighting that they reveal their most wolfish trait." The assumed "trait" is that the pack of huskies lets two huskies fight without interference until one falls, at which point "the whole band pitches upon him." As a "wolfish trait" this is utter fabrication, but as a human-influenced mecha-nism of torture and starvation in a culture of violent behavior (the pit fight, for instance) it has a sad plausibility. London's assertion should be read as more a lesson about the wolf of the human mind, the ghost wolf, than one of consistent wolf-dog behavior. This is the animal inhabiting the ultimate sym-bolic space of human evil and perversion—the cockfighting pit.

5. "A peculiarity they are remarkable for is their howling. It can be likened to nothing on land or sea. When the frost grows bitter and the aurora-borealis trails its cold fires across the heavens, they voice their misery to the night." The mythic invocations here are obvious and several. Worth noting is that London imposes misery on the howl; perhaps a safe enough assumption, given the dogs' apparent condition, but a projec-tion nonetheless. He sustains the mythic metaphor in ghostly language, comparing the howls to "a wail of lost and tortured souls" and "as though the roof had tumbled in and hell stood naked to the stars."

While *wolf-dog* means "husky" in most contexts for London, it has some flexibility. In tenets two and four above, *wolf-dog* is used more in reference to a behavioral state than as a synonym for the breed. Leaving huskies to go feral, for instance, becomes a kind of ethical tract on the hard wild, in particular vis-à-vis stealing food. A man is shot for such behavior; a dog is not only exonerated but also quietly respected for it.

London's Major Dog Stories

In this treatise on the husky we see most of the foundational assumptions behind *The Call of the Wild* and *White Fang*. In writing the piece as an essay, London writes premises, rather than possibilities to be examined as they are in fiction. Although in the comment on the "interest of man" away from wolf-dog behavior London subverts some of his credibility, he is also critiquing that interest as misplaced. Modern man, according to London, drifted away from the dogs so responsible for giving him access to "that frigid El Dorado" of the Klondike. The most obvious indicators of the essay as a progenitor for the novels include these statements: "In the annals of the country may be found the history of one dog-driver who wagered a thousand dollars that his favorite husky could start a thousand pounds on a level trail," and, "Of course it was an exceptional dog, but creatures are often measured by their extremes."

The emergence of his process through the stories and essay leads us to *The Call of the Wild*, but London would have to take one further step in order to complete his reconciliation of [English naturalist Charles] Darwin, [English philosopher Herbert] Spencer, [German philosopher Karl] Marx, and [German philosopher Friedrich] Nietzsche. He needed the twin. He needed the opposing but related figure in his mythic construct to achieve his totemic structure of the wolf-dog and the individual-versus-social being. The novel long purported (including by London himself) to contain this figure is *White Fang*, but without [his short story] "Bâtard" in the mix, London's creative process is left to a simple contrasting pair of novels that does not do that process justice.

[London biographer] Russ Kingman considered "Bâtard" to be a contrast to *The Call of the Wild* that followed a similar structure, but Jack London finally gave this role to *White Fang*, calling it an "antithesis" and ensuring that the two novels would often be published in the same volume as companion pieces. The distinctions among "Bâtard," *Call*, and *White Fang* indicate that London's process toward establishing the binary between wild and domestic was as much a complicated study of the psyche as it was a knowledgeable treatment of biological imperatives. . . . Concern over the nature of nature has lost none of its power to incite arguments about good and evil, and the literature of the wolf is brimming with such incidents. In the character Bâtard we see the full structure of London's wolf-to-dog idea, which discloses as well London's struggle with atavism and the primal self in several ways.

First, *The Call of the Wild's* main character, Buck, is made free and feral [wild]. This is called good, a return to or realization of his fundamental self, resulting in an anthem to freedom despite the hardness of the world. It's hard to tell if, according to London's worldview, all dogs possess this wolf self or if some are fundamentally bred to weakness and have lost the wild soul. One problem in London's thinking here is that a feral dog is not a wolf, and the degree of lupine [wolflike] blood's presence has only morphological bearing on fitness for life in the wild. London also makes an assumption about "the ancestral" in that the shepherd/Saint Bernard mix in Buck is somehow a ready conduit to a Platonic, ancient wolf beyond morphology. Implicit as well is the idea of Buck's potential acceptance by a pack, which is highly unlikely, indeed barely plausible.

Next, the title hero of *White Fang* is tamed and domesticated through love. This too is considered good, an earned retirement and an acceptable transference of the dominance model to civilization. According to London's system, White Fang's hybridization (one-quarter dog) renders him more justifiably, if not easily, tamed than a pure wolf. The problem is that the matter of domesticating his wolf blood has to be fitted into the same system that celebrates Buck's freedom. London's precedent is his construct of the "wolf-dog" (the husky) of the sled teams, which is at once tamed enough to work for humanity but wild enough to tough out the hard conditions of the white silence. It is a brilliantly and errantly fabricated ghost wolf.

Finally, as the linchpin between the novels, the title antihero of "Bâtard" possesses a symbiotic evil, the naturally cruel made also humanly cruel by way of directly applied human cruelty—an approach representative of naturalism's pessimistic determinism and class commentary. The friction here is *within* the malevolence model—that Bâtard is not simply called a devil because of his response to a cruel owner but has actually become or has always been inherently demonic, possessed of a soul and cunning that our narrator asserts to be born of his evil.

Which, then, is the "antithesis" to *The Call of the Wild*—*White Fang* or "Bâtard"? It seems that the binary London was trying to construct has become at least a triad: good, natural evil (which tends toward the amorality of nature), and constructed evil (which mediates the wolf and dog through both their blood and the morality projected upon them). All three stories suffer from certain assumptions of what is good for the dog or wolf, but the primordial image of wolf that surfaces in *White Fang* is not nearly the image of evil that the hybrid Bâtard becomes. London is negotiating (intuitively, it seems) the nature and nurture argument according to highly Jungian [after Swiss psychiatrist Carl Jung] methods that correct Manichean [dualistic] thought. He is negotiating as well the role that the biological wolf plays in the moral universe of his fiction.

The Primordial Howl

The Call of the Wild put Jack London on the map. The "dog story" writer grew in parallel popularity to the writer of [his later novel] *The Sea-Wolf* and novels of social commentary until, in time, the writer of the dog story won out, even at some expense to his reputation as a naturalist. *The Sea-Wolf* also acts as a bridge between the dog stories and sea adventures, linking them through the mythic connection of water and wolf analyzed in chapter 7, and is the only other canonized work of London's (*Martin Eden* and *The Iron Heel* are considered minor canonical works but are seldom cited and rarely if ever taught). The device driving *The Call of the Wild* is the "white silence" established in his earlier stories and that set the hard determinist tone of his Yukon corpus.

"The White Silence" is both a story and a label for the naturalist theme found, for instance, in [London's story] "The Law of Life" through the wolves that devour Koskoosh [the protagonist of the story]. Within this model of a massive and enveloping world without its spiritual sphere, the wolf is no more a conscious agent than is a blizzard. "It" is a force of nature certainly red in tooth and claw in its imagery but appropriate to naturalism only in its *indifference.* Cruelty is usually a nonissue, a matter of casual default in London's naturalism, except in terms of human domestication of an animal, when cruelty is critiqued from the point of view of another character or, more clinically, by a third-person narrator. The word indicates for his characters either the natural state of things or an all-too-human response to that state. But his real puzzle, which he began piecing together in his short fiction, was how to depict this force of nature as a being he knew to be possessed of life and thought, even free will.

Although he never said so directly, Jack London's work demonstrates a focused effort to understand the Fenris myth [in Norse mythology, an enormous wolf] through a combination of naturalistic determinism and atavism. He dropped into the northern white silence a super wolf, a hybrid whose dog blood would reconcile him with human culture and whose wolf blood would equip him for survival. By Zarathustra's [protagonist of Friedrich Nietzsche's *Thus Spoke Zarathustra*] way of thinking, the dog might fit the ignorant and docile condition of humanity, domesticated far from its morphological state as a wolf. In this way, according to the prophet, the wolf instructs the dog. In the Norse [mythology] context, the stakes of a wolf-dog reconciliation were no less than the end of the world. And so London is now faced with another conundrum—how transcendence must work, how the soul might exist and function in a deterministic existentialism. What he decides upon as the vehicle for this apotheosis is the nonhuman psyche, and he chooses the wolf-dog event, the human manipulation of evolutionary biology, as his departure point.

It's worth noting that the iconic status of the wolf as a totem of many indigenous Siberians and as both demonic man-eater and vermin to czarist Russians contributed to London's popularity there, which was augmented later by his socialist writings. And London's more symbolic wolf moments would be corroborated by the Freudian/Jungian interpretation that [German writer] Hermann Hesse made internationally famous and linked directly to the eastern European landscape. Hesse employed the wolf as a harrier of the questing character, replacing the monkey on the back. This shadow, the steppenwolf, assembles itself from the range of northeastern Europe to the Far East, bearing connotations of the Golden Horde and the Khans' lupine lineage, the German political division of Hesse's time, and the individual's own psychological territorial conflict. The steppenwolf was cast by Hesse as that which needed to be subdued, denied, in order for a person to have a complete and stable self. Such repression, however, paradoxically empowers the ghost wolf, makes it grow and run, hungry and hard and around the world.

The Call of the Wild and Primitivism

This is the context in which *The Call of the Wild* came to be, and through which the primordial image of the wolf gained greater fame in America. The chapter titles in *The Call of the Wild* are enough to indicate its deeply atavistic and archetypal structure; such chapters as "Into the Primitive," "The Dominant Primordial Beast," and "The Sounding of the Call" are interspersed with chapters on "law," "mastership" and "toil." London's exaggeration of the hardship in nature, the struggle for survival, clarified naturalism through Spencerianism [after philosopher Herbert Spencer]. By careful juxtaposition, the world of human cruelty simply looks "natural," determined, fated, automatic. The little latitude allowed for choice is dwarfed by images of violence and suffering. When elements of romance arise through the few people capable of demonstrating tenderness and through the basic innocence of the dog's heart, they are the more powerful for their appearance in the white silence. The combination of nature red in fang and claw with purity and self-realization added to the education in ambivalence of later generations, amounting to both the deification and the demonization of wolves.

The best edition of *The Call of the Wild* I have found is Daniel Dyer's, with its annotations and "Illustrated Reader's Companion." Dyer combines a useful and well-presented collection of photographs with a number of literary and biographical facts about London's craft (for example, that he considered the title "The Wolf" for *The Call of the Wild*; that he is credited with coining the phrase "call of the wild"; and that he used several sources on sled dogs, which Dyer lists). Dyer cites [American author] Barry Lopez and [English zoologist] Desmond Morris, rather than scientific sources, for wolf information, and he includes *The Hidden Life of Dogs*, but the bulk of the annotations tip toward place specificity and zoological history (for example, dog breeds and how they were known at the turn of the century). I have little to add to Dyer's commentary beyond recommending it and will forgo too much analysis of *The Call of the Wild*, as ultimately it is a novel about a dog. *White Fang*, however, regards a hybrid more closely related to and surrounded by wolves, and takes London's dog and wolf stories to a telling conclusion.

London's Protagonists' Quests for Individualism Are Paradoxical

Paul Deane

Paul Deane has taught at Bentley College in Boston.

In the following viewpoint, Deane discusses the theme of individualism in The Call of the Wild, *comparing Buck's quest for individuality to that of the protagonists of London's other famous novels:* White Fang, The Sea-Wolf, *and* Martin Eden. *For London, Deane writes, society paradoxically encourages individualism yet rejects those who seek to live independently. Civilization inhibits the basic nature of its members, and London's characters such as Buck, White Fang, and Martin Eden must reassert themselves if they wish to live fully. As each confronts a more primitive way of living, he regresses, yet grows. However, independence comes with a price, as Buck must live apart from society and Martin Eden commits suicide. London's ambiguous depiction of the individual ultimately speaks for itself, Deane states.*

Their interest in Jack London's naturalism and socialism has led critics and students to overlook the major intellectual conflict in London's work: the paradox of individualism. The conclusions from book to book and within books are not consistent, for London himself was never consistent, but in the very inconsistency, London revealed more about himself than he was aware.

The Individual in *The Call of the Wild*

The Call of the Wild presents the situation of a dog "socialized" into an individual, apart from society and eventually antagonistic to it. The force of society causes the development of the individual, even though Buck, in the process, is turned against society. A comfortable, upper-middle-class dog with implicit faith in the superiority of man's wisdom to his own, and reliant upon man rather than himself, Buck submits to his original kidnapping, though he dislikes being tied. He is, as London says, "an unduly civilized dog." The word "unduly" implies error, for civilization fails Buck over and over. He is beaten, whipped, and starved by those to whom he has transferred his allegiance and therewith his individuality. He has come to undervalue himself.

Yet Buck is neither weak nor stupid. "He learned quickly" how to avoid trouble, how to put himself in the best position. His basic nature, swamped, absorbed into society, and effectually negated, reasserts itself. "Instincts long dead came alive again." Like [protagonist] Humphrey Van Weyden in *The Sea-Wolf*, "his development was rapid." London's choice of word often indicates his sympathy, for though Buck is regressing to a less civilized state, he is also developing as a being distinct from others, sure of himself, confident of his own ability. Since the total impression of Buck is admirable, London here seems allied with the person, or dog, who develops and depends upon himself. Buck's alter ego, White Fang, does not come off so well.

But Buck's growing assertion of his individuality is not without qualities disturbing to his environment. The leader of the dog team, Spitz, is also an individualist, who maintains team solidarity by his superior power. Subtly Buck undermines Spitz's authority, but he also destroys the team's ability to work together as a unit. His right to do this is questionable. Spitz exists solely for himself, though by doing so, he is able to keep society together. When Buck overwhelms him, we accept his action because he is fighting for his own right, something beyond the immediate law.

John Thornton is the last link between society and Buck. The dog feels "genuine, passionate love ... for the first time." He worships Thornton, who, through his respect for Buck and for Buck's freedom, rekindles somewhat the animal's faith in man. The influence of the primitive, however, is too much for the great dog: "He was older than the days he had seen and the breaths he had drawn. He linked the past with the present, and the eternity behind him throbbed through him in a mighty rhythm ... this great love ... seemed to bespeak the soft, civilizing influence," and civilization had too often fallen short. "He knew there was no middle course. He must either master or be mastered." The test is not a fair one, for Thornton dies, leaving Buck to continue his desocialization.

White Fang

White Fang's story is the reverse of Buck's—a view of the usual course of the civilizing influence. White Fang is a wolf who is made part of society. At the end of the novel he is in the condition in which we first meet Buck: His individuality has been brought under control and made subservient to the demands of society. This bare outline is enough to indicate a change in London's point of view, for while there is a surface similarity, the effect of the two books is not at all the same. In the last view of Buck, he is admirable, true to his nature, respected; for White Fang one feels disappointment; his story is one of degradation.

As Buck heard a call from the past, White Fang, whose mother lived with the Indians, is called by her influence. It may be argued that he is conditioned to accept submission and not altogether to blame, yet he seems to choose his fate. When he sees his mother tied, he feels that "it savored of the trap, of bondage. Freedom to run and roam and lie down at will had been his heritage; and here it was being infringed upon." But when the call of the wild comes to him, he does not respond. There are at least two explicit reasons and an implicit third. White Fang is afraid of man. Gray Beaver, the Indian, beats him for any show of defiance. Like Buck, the wolf learns that a man with a club is to be obeyed. The second reason is responsible for his fear. At almost any time White Fang could have returned to the forest. He tries once, but "he arose and trotted fornlornly back to camp . . . pausing to sit down and whimper and listen to the call." He has taken the easy way, and herein lies his condemnation. "White Fang lay at Gray Beaver's feet, gazing at the fire that warmed him, blinking and dozing, secure . . . it was the placing of his destiny in another's hands, a shifting of the responsibility of existence. This in itself was compensation, for it is easier to lean upon another than to stand alone."

What are the results of placing one's fate elsewhere than upon himself? When the Indians break camp, White Fang makes a break for freedom. But his "bondage [and the word is significant, because at no time had White Fang not been at liberty to leave] had softened him. Irresponsibility had weakened him. A panic seized him and he ran madly toward the village." When he had been an individual, he had been strong, self-reliant. Now "he knew an overpowering desire for the protection and companionship of man."

But as in *The Call of the Wild* the argument for individualism does not go unchallenged. Among the other dogs White Fang is essentially alone. Within the limits of man-made society he develops his own qualities. "He could not endure the touch of another body. He must always be free, on his own legs, touching no living thing." Like Buck he rises to mastery of the other animals, but unlike Buck, who acted with the right, White Fang is wrong. He "knew the law well: to oppress the weak and obey the strong. He ate his share of the meat as rapidly as he could. And then woe the dog that had not yet finished." "He compelled them to an unremitting respect for him." "He was a monstrous tyrant. He oppressed the weak with a vengeance." Such action is that of the dictator, the ultimate individual. At this point individualism breaks down and ceases to be admirable.

What of the action of the other dogs? Because White Fang stands alone, because he is a wolf and consequently different from them, they attack him at every opportunity. "He was the wild, the unknown, the terrible, the ever-menacing." Society is quick to suppress and punish departures from the norms it sets up.

The Sea-Wolf

The Sea-Wolf presents the points of view of both *The Call of the Wild* and *White Fang* in such a complete balance that the result is almost a synthesis of their themes. External comparison is inadequate, for only in Humphrey Van Weyden is there anything like White Fang or Buck. Van Weyden, through association with a less civilized society, regresses to a more primitive state, though he does not go so far as Buck. London's most complete individual, [sea captain and antagonist] Wolf Larsen, differs only in physical ability at the end of the book from the way he is shown at the beginning.

Like White Fang, Larsen is isolated by his individuality from the rest of the crew (society). But the picture is a more penetrating view of what complete independence means. "He is certainly an individual of the most pronounced type," Van Weyden says, "but he is very lonely. There is no congeniality between him and the rest of the men aboard ship." Later he adds, "The loneliness of the man is slowly being borne in upon me. There is not a man aboard but hates and fears him, nor is there a man whom he does not despise." The book invites comparison with [Herman Melville's] *Moby-Dick* and Wolf Larsen with Ahab [a character in *Moby-Dick*]. In Larsen one is conscious of "a tremendous and excessive mental or spiritual strength that lay behind, sleeping in the depths of his being." Like Ahab, he has a fundamental lack: in Ahab the lack is represented by his ivory leg and his scar; in Larsen, by his frequent debilitating headaches. Like Ahab, too, "he was daring destiny, and he was unafraid."

Larsen and Ahab are completely independent persons, self-involved and society excluded. As owner of the *Ghost* Larsen has a responsibility toward his crew, yet the ship and all her hands exist solely for the whim of the captain. Like White Fang he rules by strength, "a strength we are wont to associate with things primitive . . . a strength savage, ferocious, alive in itself." His strength and individualism go hand in hand. He is the ultimate source of justice because he is strong and depends on no one; he allows no one to interpret justice for him. "Might is right and that is all there is to it," he says. "Weakness is wrong . . . it is good for oneself to be strong and evil for oneself to be weak." The basic question remains: Does he have the right to act as he does? Can any great work in any field be produced except by a person who has dared to go beyond the safety of society's limits and sanctions? Larsen and Ahab both establish a totalitarian context in which all other rights are submerged and made inferior to theirs. When Larsen and Van Weyden discuss [John Milton's epic] *Paradise Lost*, the captain champions the cause of Lucifer: "Lucifer was a free spirit. To serve was to suffocate. He preferred suffering in freedom to serving in servility. He did not care to serve God. He cared to serve nothing. He stood on his own legs. He was an individual."

Larsen is heroic in his way also, for he does fear nothing. Confident of his own abilities, he depends on them, and he is secure in them. But what of Humphrey Van Weyden? He is a society poet, existing in and for society, without the qualifications of a true artist, those of independence upon himself and his abilities to understand and face life. When his ferry is sunk, he says, "I was alone, floating in the midst of a grey primordial vastness, I confess a madness seized me, that I shrieked aloud as the women had done, and beat the water with my numb hands." He is afraid to be alone, for having never been so, he has had no chance to test his abilities; he does not know what he is, what he is capable of. Yet of the two men, Van Weyden is the more socially acceptable and desirable. The contest between him and Larsen would seem to be an unfair one, and from the physical point of view it is. But London gives the two men approximately equal intellects. If Larsen's is the more daring and adventuresome, Van Weyden's is the better disciplined. This is his one advantage and the thing that allows him to triumph over the captain, though he never defeats him.

In the presence of brutality and a more basic form of existence, Van Weyden regresses, although, at the same time, like Buck, he grows. He is given a chance to use his body and to develop an aspect of life different from the intellectual. Here he has another advantage over Larsen, for while the mind of both men remain essentially as capable for most of the book, Van Weyden is growing stronger physically as Larsen is being weakened by paresis [partial paralysis]. Moreover, physical development opens an area to Van Weyden that had always been apparent to Larsen, and because the writer is intelligent, he can appreciate what it has to offer. Just as Ishmael [the narrator of *Moby-Dick*] grows as a result of his experience aboard the [sailing vessel] *Pequod*, Van Weyden grows in understanding primarily through association with an individual. "While my faith in human life still survived Wolf Larsen's destructive criticism, he had nevertheless been the cause of change in minor matters. He had opened up for me the world of the real . . . from which I had always shrunk. I learned to look more closely at life as it was lived . . . and to recognize that there were such things as facts in the world, to emerge from the realm of mind and ideas." He has left the ways of thinking which his class considers acceptable and right. He is able to think for himself, and his "wild desire to vindicate [himself] in Wolf Larsen's eyes" is accomplished in the last melodramatic chapters after the *Ghost* has been wrecked and Larsen incapacitated. His rise is more than a physical one. His regression has not taken him so far into the purely animalistic as Larsen has gone, and he is able to retain enough of his former sensitivity to appreciate the value of his experience. His spiritual and intellectual change enables him to surpass Larsen, for the poet keeps, as he says, the faith in human life that Larsen lacked. He is able to go on to a realization of the true function of the individual and apply his discoveries and abilities for the use of society.

Although London's sympathy is with Larsen in the sense of his magnificent physique, it is clear that sheer strength is not enough; the individual's powers must be properly applied. Satan is the most completely developed character in *Paradise Lost*, but he does not triumph in that poem.

Martin Eden

Martin Eden chronicles on the intellectual level, as *White Fang* did on the physical, the growth of a primitive, a giant in size, strength, and endurance, into a giant intellectually. But *Martin Eden* goes beyond the story of the wolf and indicates what happens when Martin continues to grow until he is as far beyond society as he was when he was ignorant.

Love for Ruth Morse [his cultured girlfriend], a desire to be worthy of her, to understand the things that she and her class take for granted, prompt him to study. "He was enobled by the loftiness of thought and beauty he found in the books. This led him to believe . . . that, up and above him, in society . . . all men and women thought these thoughts and lived them." He finds, perhaps inevitably, that they do not. He finds, indeed, that society's chief value is the financial return that education can produce; when he begins to write, Ruth and her family continually ask him when his writing will be successful, when he will settle down to "normal," in short, when his education will begin to pay off.

As Martin turned his back on his own class and alienated himself from it, eventually his desire to discover truth and to remain true to himself alienates him from the class he sought to enter. Eventually he goes beyond all classes and faces the loneliness of individual man, the loneliness that Van Weyden indicated in Wolf Larsen. "He was disappointed in it all. He had developed into an alien. He had exiled himself." As a writer he finds that society, which glorifies the great individuals of literature and history, wants no part of an author who does not fit the pattern of comfortable social ideals. In the very class which he feels should understand individuality, he finds "narrow little formulas, herd creatures, flocking together and patterning their lives by one another's opinions, failing of being individuals."

In his search for knowledge, Martin is led to attend some socialist meetings. Although he is impressed by the amount of genuine scholarship he finds, he is too much of an individual to subscribe to an ideology that de-emphasizes the value of each person. "As for myself, I am an individualist. I believe the race is to the swift, the battle to the strong. Individualism is the hereditary and eternal foe of socialism."

Yet despite his exaltation of the individual, despite his condemnation of society's sheep-like attitude, London causes Martin, who is not a sheep, to commit suicide. Unable to adjust to a world which has disappointed him, and unable to return to the class from which he originally came, completely isolated, Martin drowns himself. As in the previous books, there is a balance of attitudes. London's appraisal of the status of the individual in and against society allows no general conclusion and the paradox remains. Perhaps the balance speaks for itself.

Contemporary Perspectives on Wildness

Out of the Wilderness

Jerry Adler

Jerry Adler has been a contributing editor at Newsweek *and The* Daily Beast, *where he writes about medicine, science, and ideas. He is the author of* High Rise: How 1,000 Men and Women Worked Around the Clock for Five Years and Lost $200 Million Building a Skyscraper.

Although getting out into the wild has generally been considered a desirable goal, Adler reports in the following viewpoint that fewer people are doing so in the twenty-first century. The lack of interest in nature has been attributed to the rise of video games and the Internet, but not, surprisingly, to television. There is a concern that if a generation of young people never gets outdoors, they will lose their fascination with, and caring for, the natural world. However, Adler does not seem worried. If anything, he writes, it is now nearly impossible to find a spot in nature to be alone: The most famous places are habitually clogged with tourists. It would be nice to get children out into the wild, he concludes, but maybe it is also beneficial to give nature a chance to heal itself.

In wildness is the preservation of the World. So wrote [American author Henry David] Thoreau, back when there was plenty of wildness and little reason to think that the world might someday be in need of preserving. Wilderness was a place most people shunned in the 1850s, back before the invention of most of the things that made it even slightly habitable, such as Gore-Tex jackets and aluminum tent poles. But Thoreau's romantic ideal of nature has lived on in the American imagination, even as the reality of it—a place without bathtubs, just when you are most likely to be in need of one—has become almost unimaginably remote from our daily immersion in climate-controlled, hygienic luxury. Yet now that ideal is threatened—according to a study published in *Proceedings of the National Academy of Sciences [of the United States]*—by a "fundamental and pervasive shift" since at least the 1980s away from the activity known to Thoreau as "walking in the woods," now designated "nature-based recreation." The study—not coincidentally funded by the Nature Conservancy—warns of a danger Thoreau could not foresee: that the natural world cannot be saved if people aren't willing to set foot in it.

The authors, conservation biologists Oliver Pergams of the University of Illinois at Chicago and Patricia Zaradic, paint a picture of America seriously at odds with our national self-image. Pergams and Zaradic found declines averaging about 1 percent a year in per capita participation in the most significant outdoor activities, notably camping and hunting. A small increase in backpacking did little to offset the overall picture, because hardly anyone does it in the first place. Participation in duck hunting, which for obscure bureaucratic reasons is tracked separately from other kinds of hunting, is off 60 percent from its peak, which was back in 1953. Even fishing is down sharply, except in commercials for mutual funds and retirement communities. Visiting a national park, says Zaradic, "used to be the iconic American family vacation, something Americans did, on average, once a year. Now we're even turning away from that."

What could cause such a profound shift in sensibilities? In a 2006 paper, Pergams and Zaradic performed an elaborate statistical analysis correlating numerous social variables with national-park visits, and found that almost the entire decline could be attributed to increases since 1987 in video games, Internet usage, movie viewing (and the price of gasoline). Oddly,

A new study finds that people are not getting out into nature as much as they used to. Camping has fallen by the wayside as the younger generation prefers to stay indoors playing video games and surfing the Internet. © David Epperson/Getty Images.

the list does not include television, which was entrenched in the culture long before outdoor recreation began declining in the 1980s.

The implications the authors draw are dire. "There's a pretty direct pathway from exposure to nature, especially as a child, to caring about it," says Pergams. So along with obesity and attention-deficit disorder, you can now, if you choose, blame video games for the greenhouse effect.

But is the problem really that too many people are staying home from the wilderness? Some, presumably including Thoreau, would say that the last thing nature needs is more people in it. "I have," he wrote in *Walden*, "my own sun and moon and stars, and a little world all to myself." In 1850 he was able to find this a few miles outside Boston, but just let him try to duplicate it in Yellowstone [National] Park, say, on Memorial Day weekend. Or in Los Glaciares National Park in Argentina's Patagonia region, to which Dominique Browning, a New York editor, made an arduous and expensive pilgrimage recently. In an op-ed piece in the *New York Times*, she described her trip as a disappointing vista of litter glimpsed between the heads of boorish tourists while the boat's soundtrack echoed among the majestic glaciers. The experience left her, she says, with an appreciation of "the coffee-table book as a mode of travel." The wilderness looks best through the lens of a professional photographer, who can crop the plastic bags out of the trees.

The study didn't consider snowmobiles, all-terrain vehicles or other motorized forms of "nature-based recreation," but Zaradic thinks they deserve a place in the wilderness, too, as long as they get people to the out-of-doors. This is, of course, a fairly controversial position in the environmental movement. Her faith in the transformative power of nature is impressive. It would be nice to get kids into the woods once in a while so they can learn, at least, how to swat a mosquito. But maybe we'd all do better to give the World a break from us, so it can heal on its own.

Modern Attitudes Toward Wolves in the Wild Vary Greatly

Economist

The Economist *is a weekly newsmagazine with a focus on international politics and business news and opinion.*

In the following viewpoint, the Economist *provides an overview of the modern debate about wolf population in Europe and America. For centuries, wolves were seen as a great enemy to humans and were consequently exterminated. However, modern attitudes toward the wolf have changed, and the wolf has gained protection from conservationists. Urban liberals see in the wolf a vestige of an older, wilder, and freer environment. Their views contrast with rural farmers who suffer great monetary damage to their herds. Today, control of the wolf population in Europe and America has become a political issue that must be handled carefully.*

In August 2011 Desiree Versteeg, a Dutch mortuarist, was driving home in the suburbs of Arnhem in the eastern Netherlands when she saw an animal in the road. "At first I thought it was a dog. Then I thought it was a fox. Then—I couldn't believe my eyes—I saw it was a wolf." She got out of the car to take a picture. "I was seven or eight metres away from him. He couldn't get away because a fence was blocking his path. He turned and stared at me. That was a frightening moment." Both she and the wolf fled.

From Ms Versteeg's photographs, and from the carcass of a deer found nearby—its throat torn out in classic wolf fashion—scientists verified that she was the first person to have seen a wolf in the Netherlands since 1897. Having talked to the experts, she now understands that the wolf was probably more frightened than she was. "But all you know at the time is it's a wolf, it's a predator and I'm in its way."

Ms Versteeg's experience illustrates a dramatic reversal that has taken place in the West over the past couple of decades. Economic change has led to a fundamental shift in humanity's attitude to wolves. For the first time since man first sharpened a spear, he has stopped trying to exterminate them and taken to protecting them instead. The effort has been so successful that wolves are recolonising areas from which they disappeared as much as a century ago. As they do so, they are forging revealing divisions over whether mankind can live side by side with the species it replaced as the Western world's top predator.

State vs. Wolf

Most man-made extinctions have been accidental—the result of overhunting, or importing predators or diseases. Wolves are different. Through most of human history, killing them has been regarded as a public good. As soon as anything that looked like a state developed, it set about exterminating wolves.

In England King Edgar imposed an annual tribute of 300 wolf skins on Idwal, king of Wales, in 960; monarchs made land grants on condition that the beneficiaries carried out wolf hunts; King Edward I employed a wolf-hunter-in-chief to clear central and western England of wolves. By the end of the 15th century they seem to have disappeared from England, though in Scotland they hung on a little longer: in 1563 Mary Queen of Scots had 2,000 Highlanders drive the woods of Atholl for a hunt that bagged 360 deer and five wolves.

America's original settlers, then, had no previous experience of wolves. The dense lupine population in the forests along the eastern seaboard in the New World, for which the colonists' livestock was a walking buffet, made a tough life harder still. Towns set generous bounties for wolves. In 1643 in Ipswich, Massachusetts, for instance, the reward for killing a wolf in a trap was five shillings; for killing one with a dog, it was 20s. Colonists devised imaginative ways of getting rid of them: John Josselyn, an English traveller, reported that locals would tie two fish hooks together, dip them in tallow, and leave them out for wolves to swallow.

Boston's last specimen was killed in 1657, but elsewhere on the East Coast wolves lived on in enclaves through the 18th century. Farther west they remained a serious threat for much longer. In 1848, shortly after the Mormons arrived in Salt Lake Valley, Thomas Bullock reported that "the wolves made things hideous with their continuous howls"; in 1850, 15% of Utah's budget went on wolf bounties. In the 20th century the federal government took on the job, and by 1970—largely through the use of poison—had wiped wolves out everywhere except Alaska and a pocket of northern Minnesota.

In western Europe, being hunted to death was not wolves' only problem: They also suffered from shrinking habitat. As the human population rose, people chopped down the forests for firewood and ate the deer and boar on which the wolves had fed. As they lost out in the tussle with people, wolves were exterminated, progressively, from the Benelux countries, France, Switzerland, Norway, Sweden, Denmark and West Germany. Small numbers survived in Italy and Spain.

Then sometime in the mid to late 20th century, things started to change. In Europe urbanisation, industrialisation and rising incomes led peasants to abandon their farms and move to cities. Land that had once been converted from heath or forest to fields reverted to its wild state. In some places—such as Alpine areas, where trees help protect people from avalanches—governments encouraged reforestation. The process is still going on: In the past two decades the forested area of western Europe has increased by around 7%.

At the same time as habitat suitable for wolves expanded, so did the food supply. These days people eat from supermarket shelves rather than from the land, so deer and wild boar are no longer shot for the pot. Hunters' groups have helped restore the populations of these animals, and more quarry for hunters also means more food for wolves.

It wasn't just the physical environment that was changing. On both sides of the Atlantic, attitudes were shifting too.

The Howl of Nature

Although man domesticated his best friend from the species at least 15,000 years ago, he has long regarded the wolf as his worst enemy. The wolf prowls through stories—Red Riding Hood, Peter and the Wolf, the Norse myth of the beast that will swallow the sun at Ragnarok [Norse apocalypse]—as the embodiment of evil.

In a way, it is odd that the wolf should be mankind's bête noire. Bears, which get far better press, are more dangerous. Disturb a bear and it may turn on you; disturb a wolf and it will run away. Presumably competition explains this ancient hatred. Once people took to raising animals, wolves competed with them more directly than any other creature. A pack of wolves will happily kill hundreds of sheep in an hour. In communities whose livelihood goes about on four legs, wolves and people are not compatible.

This rivalry has spawned awful cruelty. In 1814 John James Audubon, one of America's great naturalists, recorded watching a farmer in Ohio hoist trapped wolves out of a pit he had dug for them and, for his and Audubon's amusement, cut their tendons and set his dogs upon them to see how long they would last. Audubon regarded it as fine entertainment.

Yet around the middle of the 20th century sentiment started to change. First came a shift in conservationist thinking, illustrated by the life and writings of Aldo Leopold, father of the American environmental movement.

American conservationist and ecologist Aldo Leopold pioneered the modern ecology movement with his book A Sand County Almanac, *published posthumously in 1949, and inspired environmental activists in the 1960s and 70s. AP Images.*

In the 19th and early 20th centuries environmentalists believed that because predators killed other animals, conservation was best served by killing them—a view that fit the economic imperative of the times. Leopold, employed by the [United States] Forest Service to kill wolves and other predators in New Mexico, was part of that effort.

But he grew concerned about the consequences of this campaign. In *A Sand County Almanac*, first published in 1949 and probably the best-selling environmentalist book ever, he wrote, "I have watched the face of many a newly wolfless mountain, and seen the south-facing slopes wrinkle with a maze of new deer trails. I have seen every edible bush and seedling browsed, first to anaemic desuetude, and then to death. I have seen every edible tree defoliated to the height of a saddlehorn." The campaign to destroy wolves, he believed, was destroying America's landscape.

Conservationists were not the only ones who began to reconsider. So did the general public. As people moved to towns, attitudes to nature moved from utilitarian to romantic.

In America the idea of manifest destiny—that conquering territory previously controlled by savages and wild beasts was a moral duty—fell out of favour. Growing evidence of environmental damage fuelled the belief that while mankind was busy getting rich, it was ruining its most precious asset. Progress came to seem like the opposite. And as the world turned upside down, so vermin became victim. "Wolves are the antithesis of civilisation," says Doug Smith, head of the wolf programme at Yellowstone National Park. "They represent the wilderness we have lost."

Conservation Efforts

In Europe, according to Marie-Odile Guth, former director of nature conservation at the French environment ministry, wolves arouse feelings not so much of guilt as of longing. "People are tired of urban life. The wolf represents a return to natural life. It's attractive, and at the same time it's a little bit frightening." Thus economic development has both enhanced the wolf's charms and put an end to the competition that once set mankind against it.

Changing public attitudes brought legislation—in America the Endangered Species Act of 1973, in Europe the Bern Convention of 1979 and the Habitats Directive of 1992—designed to prevent the extinction of the many species that were under the cosh. And in America the idea of reintroducing wolves to Yellowstone took hold. Proposed by conservationists, it turned out to have widespread popular support; so in 1995, 14 grey wolves were captured in Canada and released in Yellowstone and nearby Idaho.

In Europe, encouraged by a combination of protection and mankind's retreat to the cities, the wolves returned naturally. They spread across the Alps from Italy into France, where the first was spotted in 1992; from Finland into Sweden, where they were identified in 1977; from Poland to Germany in the 1990s, and thence, in 2011, to the Netherlands and Belgium.

The wolves were not alone in benefiting from the legislation and the landscape changes. Other large predators started to recover too. The lynx, endangered in Europe, is now recovering fast. America's grizzly bear population has grown from 500 in the 1970s to 1,500 now. Brown bears are clinging on in some bits of western Europe, such as the Pyrenees [between France and Spain], and flourishing in other parts, such as Sweden, where the population has risen from 370 in 1966 to 3,500 now.

Compared with slow-moving bears, wolves are adaptable, adventurous creatures that breed and spread fast. Their packs operate over a territory of 250–400 square kilometres; fully grown pups leave the pack and travel up to 1,000km in search of their own territory and a mate. Using their DNA, which can be extracted from their scat, and radio-tracking collars, scientists have logged some extraordinary journeys. A wolf from southwest of Turin [Italy] lived around Bonn [Switzerland] for a year; two Italian wolves were found to be living in the Pyrenees; a Slovenian [central European] wolf travelled through Austria and into Italy where he eventually settled down with a mate near Verona. Italians were entranced by the romance of their lupine Romeo and Juliet—which came to a sad end when the female was run over by a car.

Wolf numbers are now growing in most of western Europe. But the population rebound is most dramatic in America, where the combination of protection and a sparse human population suits them perfectly. In the Rocky Mountains, since the wolf's reintroduction in 1995, the population has grown to 1,700–2,000; in the Great Lakes, where it never entirely disappeared, it has gone from 750 to 4,000 over the same period.

Some scientists credit the wolf with a dramatic ecological impact. Yellowstone's elk population has fallen from about 20,000 before the wolves arrived to 5,000 now. Bison and beavers are thriving on the resulting vegetation. The grizzly bears that scavenge the wolf kills are having a fine time. Willow and aspen have recovered along the banks of rivers; as the bushes grow into trees, the songbirds that like to live in them are flourishing.

Yet outside nature reserves the wolf's ecological effects are blurred by man, and the case for protecting it must be made on other grounds. "It's a bit like gender equality," says Guillaume Chapron of the Grimso Wildlife Research Station in Sweden. "We support it not because it is economically efficient, but because we are a modern society which believes that women should have the same rights as men. Similarly, we believe that a modern wealthy society can share its landscape with other species."

Not everybody agrees. Where humans were once united in their determination to eradicate the wolf, they are now sharply divided over its return.

Bobos in Love

On both sides of the Atlantic the wolf's supporters are in a majority. They include disproportionate numbers of young people, women and city dwellers. By and large, the farther away people live from wolves, the more they like them. The big exception is Native Americans, who live close to them and respect them. Wolves feature in their mythology as man's creator or brother and, according to Chris McGeshick of the Mole Lake Band of the Chippewa tribe in the Great Lakes area, the Indians see their fate as linked to the wolf's: "We're doing better, we're exercising our rights, we're getting back to where we were before the Europeans arrived. As the wolf gets stronger, so do the tribal people."

Environmental and animal welfare organisations are leading the fight to keep the wolf protected. They have generous supporters, for whom the wolf is totemic. When Defenders of Wildlife polls its 1m members about the species they care about, the wolf always comes out on top, according to Jamie Rappaport Clark, its president and a former director of the federal government's Fish and Wildlife Service (FWS). That makes lobbying for the wolf a priority: "Our members expect a return on their investment."

But the wolf's supporters do not care for it as much as its opponents hate it, and they have good reason to. In 2009, the worst year for her since the wolf's reintroduction, Kim Baker, a rancher in Montana, suffered seven confirmed wolf kills, 12 heads of cattle missing and yearlings that, worn down by harassment, weighed in at an average of 710lb (322kg) instead of the expected 770lb. She calculates the total losses that year at around $42,000. "Sometimes it gets pretty doggone depressing. If you could see what the wolves leave. . . . We don't raise our cattle to be tortured." Photographs show savaged dogs and cattle with their rumps chewed off. Ranchers get compensation for losses; but Ms Baker says that, because of the difficulty of proving that a wolf was to blame, the payoffs make up for only 10% of her losses.

In Europe conflict between wolves and farmers has been sharpest in France, where heavy subsidies still sustain agriculture in marginal areas. Joseph Jouffrey, president of the shepherds' association in the Hautes-Alpes, says that one of his neighbours recently lost 67 sheep. Around 5,000 were killed by wolves in the whole of France last year, up from around 1,500 five years ago. As in America, farmers say the compensation does not cover their losses. There have been anti-wolf demonstrations and arson attacks in the national park where they first appeared, and death threats against the park's staff.

In the fight against the wolves, hunters tend to side with the ranchers and shepherds. Moose hunting in Sweden is an important part of rural life, says Gunnar Gloersen, a hunter from Värmland in mid-Sweden. Every year 100,000 moose are shot, partly to protect pine trees, whose young shoots moose eat, and partly for sport. Even the schools and the police stations close on a moose-hunting day. Wolves disrupt shooting by slaughtering around 5,000–10,000 moose a year and, more importantly, by killing hunting dogs. The costs of losing a dog are not just emotional: a well-trained jämthund is worth [euro] 10,000 ($13,000). The presence of wolves reduces the value of hunting rights and, according to Mr Gloersen, costs landowners in his part of Sweden around [euro] 50m [million] a year.

The division between the wolves' opponents and supporters is cultural as well as economic. While supporters regard themselves as caring for the planet, opponents see themselves as in touch with the earth. Pierre de Boisguilbert, the general secretary of France's Société de Vènerie (hunting with hounds), characterises the wolf's supporters as "bobos"— bourgeois-bohemians, a disparaging term for urban left-wingers. "The bobos love the wolf. They'll never see one, but the idea of the wolf is great."

A Political Struggle

In America, the argument over the wolf's protected status escalated into a full-blown political battle. Wolf numbers swiftly hit the FWS's (modest) target of 100 wolves per state, so in 2002 it started talking about removing their protection. To stop this from happening, the environmental and animal rights organisations took the federal government to court. As judges deliberated, and more cases were brought, the wolf population rocketed, and hunters and ranchers got increasingly angry. In 2011 Congress lost patience and legislated to override the courts and "delist" the wolves. They are now fair game in all the Rocky Mountains and Great Lakes states where they are present.

What will happen to America's wolf population is not clear. The states are trying to cut their numbers to the FWS's original targets. Some conservationists think populations of those sizes are too small to be sustainable, and that the wolf risks being wiped out again; others say the animals are now too numerous to be culled to the target levels. Dave Mech, senior research scientist with the United States Geological Survey, says the wolf population is too large to be controlled by "fair-chase" hunting (without the use of aircraft or poison). What is clearer is the damage that the explosion of wolf numbers has done to conservation, by turning those whose livelihoods have suffered against environmental legislation. "Our biggest enemy," says Ms Baker, the rancher, "has been the Endangered Species Act."

In Europe wolves still receive strict protection from the EU [European Union] Habitats Directive. The commission took Finland to court in 2005 for allowing too much hunting, and is now pursuing a similar case against Sweden, although there is widespread recognition that the wolf's growing numbers are a problem. Culling is allowed only in tiny numbers: In France, for instance, 11 wolves may be harvested this year. Yet they have spread as far west as the Massif Central [in south-central France], where there are lots of people, and lots of sheep. "If the wolves get there in significant numbers, it will be a nightmare," says Luigi Boitani, head of the International Union for Conservation of Nature's working group on large carnivores in Europe.

Mankind's relationship with the wolf has always been difficult, and lupine politics must be delicately managed. But although this divisive canine still has too many enemies for its survival to be taken for granted, history is on its side. In most of the world, agriculture's share of economic output is shrinking, the rural population is falling and people are drifting ever farther from the soil. These days wolves are little more to most humans than a reminder of a wilder past they have put behind them, but which still tugs at their souls.

A Woman Needs a Wild Side

Suzanne Paola

Suzanne Paola teaches at Western Washington University. She is the author of Body Toxic: An Environmental Memoir *and several books of poetry.*

In the following viewpoint, Paola recounts her early years as a high school dropout and drug user, stating that while she is not proud of some of her actions, her rebel past has figured prominently in creating the woman she is today. After dropping out of high school, Paola earned a general equivalency diploma (GED) and enrolled in a community college, falling in love with literature. She went on to become a "good girl" and a professor. However, she often uses knowledge gained from her early years to counsel students, protest injustice, and even argue with corporations over the phone. Paola recognizes that her wild side now forms one-half of a well-rounded personality.

I have an indelible memory, like a swipe of ink, of the day I walked into the high school I'd quit two years before. I was there to take the GED [general equivalency diploma] exam. I arrived in my uniform of melted-on jeans, thick Jersey Girl makeup and[—]hard to believe now, given my fanatical love of animals[—]my prized rabbit-fur jacket. I hunched my shoulders under the glare of the assistant principal, a man with a military build and a deeply cut scowl. As a student, I'd cut class and used drugs, any kind of drugs. I'm sure I had made his life miserable.

A Bad Girl

I was a bad girl from an industrial town. My boyfriends didn't flip burgers but dealt drugs; a few carried knives and other weapons, accessories of a dicey lifestyle. Even among the worst of the blue-collar kids, I stood out, reeking of pot and dropping acid in class. As a young adolescent, I had always been mildly smart and unpopular, and I started high school with the overwhelming urge to get out of that rut. This was a time when many people my age felt that parents, the government and much of traditional society had made a mess of our world with [the war in] Vietnam (not to mention [the political scandal] Watergate). Nothing made sense; boys I knew were being sent to war courtesy of a bizarre lottery decreed by a shifty-eyed, perspiring president [Richard Nixon]. On the news, images of body bags sparked protests with sometimes brutal results, as at Kent State [University in Ohio], where four students were killed by the National Guard.

Maybe that's why, on the first day of high school, I felt scared but then quickly thrilled, when I found a girl groaning against the wall in the bathroom. "Too much acid, too little sleep," diagnosed another kid. At first, I thought they were talking about OD'ing [overdosing] on coffee, but it was clear that the girls' bathroom was pungent with knowledge, a threshold to the dangerous world of adulthood. I resolved to belong. I was done with being a good girl and I began pleading for bathroom passes as if I had no bladder, learning to suck in sweet marijuana in the stalls.

"Don't become one of those bathroom girls," a nice teacher urged me. But it was too late. Soon, those bathroom girls were my friends and I found myself a boyfriend, too, a guy who sold pot and psychedelics. Together, we drank, did speed and huffed a cleaning fluid called Carbona from paper bags.

Eventually, I quit going to classes, then dropped out altogether. My parents begged me to stop using drugs, then threw up their hands and gave up on me. Things might have continued that way if I hadn't overdosed on methadone. I'd used other narcotics before, including heroin, but this experience left me vomiting and wrecked on the floor for a week straight.

While I was recovering, my so-called friends, including the boyfriend, made themselves scarce. Once I was better, I never heard from them again.

Turning My Life Around

Scared off drugs, I turned to the one talent I'd emerged with from the few classes I'd attended in high school: typing. I worked as a secretary for a year, got bored staring at a typewriter all day and tried community college. Once there, I was smitten with [Shakespeare's] *Hamlet* and [American poet] Emily Dickinson and writing. I'd always kept a diary, no matter how drug-addled I was. Now I couldn't stop coming out with poems and stories. After earning my GED, I transferred to a four-year college, paying my way by typing in summers. Then I went to graduate school in creative writing.

I met my future husband in poetry class. He'd also had a difficult childhood, and we instinctively understood one another, opening up in a way we hadn't with anyone else. We both knew what it was like to keep parts of ourselves hidden.

Meanwhile, I found myself morphing hopelessly into a good girl, full of fear that my younger self would be found out. I did all my assignments early and never risked bothering anyone with questions. Even once I was working as a professor, if the subject of drugs came up, I acted as if I'd never heard of them. I thought of my bad-girl history as something apart from me, an alter ego in rabbit fur. Only my husband knew the truth.

Of course, I'd sometimes slip up, telling a friend, for instance, that crank and crystal meth were the same thing. "How do you know?" was the always-amused reply. I'd mumble something about how drugs were everywhere in New Jersey in 1973 (implication: even in the life of a good kid like me). Then I'd change the topic. I worried that if my friends knew the kind of people I'd once spent time with, they wouldn't want me around.

One time, deep into my good-girl phase of life, my husband and I arrived home to our new rental to find my spotted mutt listing to the side and whimpering. We rushed her to the vet, who concluded that she must have ingested traces of some kind of narcotic (presumably left behind by the previous tenant). He gave her saline and released her[—]no big deal[—]but driving home, when I saw a police car a block from our duplex, I started crying and insisted that my husband keep driving. I was sure the vet could read my past somehow and had called the cops.

Harnessing One's Wild Side

I could have ended up stuck in that place of shame, keeping that bad girl locked in her den of iniquity, if I hadn't written a memoir in which I used her voice. I didn't set out to invoke her. I was looking through my old notebooks in which I'd once scribbled my thoughts. The girl in those pages sounded defiant in the face of powers that napalmed the Vietnamese and corporations that dumped toxic chemicals onto lands that fed public wells. (The area of northern New Jersey where I grew up had led the United States in the number of hazardous-waste sites.) The more I read her outraged voice, the more I began to welcome her into my adult life. In my teaching, too, I discovered that there were plenty of "bad" kids like me, kids who needed someone who understood what it took to cross over to good without losing themselves. In my classes, I encouraged these students, some former users, to write down their feelings, urging, "Don't let anyone tell you your story doesn't count."

I've also conjured the bad girl in other places. In the late 1970s, when the prospect of granting women equality was an inflammatory one, I rang doorbells to garner support for the Equal Rights Amendment. "What kind of girl wants to use a men's bathroom?" men would yell. Decades later, I've become quite the protestor. I still live in a world that sometimes doesn't make sense, one that calls out for justice. My husband, son (then 5) and I demonstrated against the invasion of Iraq, at candlelight vigils and on street corners. I've counseled rape survivors and joined a group that combats AIDS in Africa.

All of which has helped me realize that my inner bad girl is an essential part of me[—]only instead of taking drugs, I try to shake up what society has come to think of as acceptable but isn't. My noisy, rebellious side gets results. When my very courteous Southern husband can't elicit a response from a recalcitrant customer-service rep, he calls me over and says, "Honey, would you Yankee 'em for me?" I'll grab the phone, and whoever the person is, I won't hang up until she has been appropriately Yankee'd. I may yell, as I did after we had to take our very sick son to the emergency room and our insurer refused to pay. Each time I called the surly claims representative, I told her, "I'm not going away." And I didn't. I went straight to the state insurance commissioner, who sent the company a letter. After that, our claims whizzed through so fast we joked that we could charge dinners out on our insurance card and not get an argument.

Because of moments like that, I've stopped feeling shame over my younger self. I now see her as my first step toward strength: misguided, sure, but real, ferocious and female. In truth, we probably could have afforded to cover our son's ER visit, but I like to think that my persistence might make it easier for other families who don't have the money to pay their medical bills. Maybe that's what protesting is about[—]communicating what you know of being down-and-out to the larger world.

There's no need for my good-girl side in the bedroom, either. Dutiful, she has nothing to do with pleasure. Though my bad girl may have begun her pursuit of sensuality going in some wrong directions, she has always been interested in her body, in showing it, testing it out. She simply needed a better outlet[—]and what could be better than nurturing my relationship with the man I love? Bring on the mascara and the Steppenwolf [rock band that sang "Born to Be Wild"]. As a girl, I dreamed of such a life: of being a published writer; a mother; and a well-loved wife. How strange to have gotten everything I wanted.

If I could go back to high school, I'd tell that vice principal, the man who intimidated me so, that after years of being suppressed, my shadow bad girl has earned a place in my consciousness, ready to form half of a well-balanced whole. I can be law-abiding yet still reap I-don't-take-no-for-an-answer results. The girl of the rabbit fur is a symbol, yes, but she is also an acknowledgment that although I didn't channel my teenage anger in the best way possible, anger has its uses. It's comforting to know that my ferocity is inside me, protecting me and my family from harm.

Wildness Inspires Freedom and Integrity

bell hooks

bell hooks is a Kentucky native who has taught at Berea College. She is the author of more than thirty books, and her recent work focuses on issues of social class, race, and gender.

In the following viewpoint, hooks (the lower case is purposeful) recounts her youth growing up in what would now be referred to as "Appalachia," as a so-called "hillbilly." However, neither of these terms were used by her own people, who displayed a fierce pride in their own wild lifestyle. hooks suggests that she owes much of what she now values in her adult personality—her independence, integrity, and critical consciousness—to her Kentucky upbringing and the freedoms that went along with that culture. She claims that those wild Appalachian values imprinted themselves on her at an early age and provided the framework according to which she still lives.

Sublime silence surrounds me. I have walked to the top of the hill, plopped myself down to watch the world around me. I have no fear here, in this world of trees, weeds—and growing things. This is the world I was born into—a world of wild things. In it the wilderness in me speaks. I am wild. I hear my elders caution mama, telling her that she is making a mistake, letting me "run wild," letting me run with my brother as though no gender separates us. We are making our childhood together in Kentucky hills, experiencing the freedom that comes from living away from civilization. Even as a child I knew that to be raised in the country, to come from the

bell hooks, "Free Spirits: A Legacy of Wildness," *Appalachian Heritage*, Summer 2008, vol. 36, no. 3, pp. 37–39.

backwoods left one without meaning or presence. Growing up we did not use terms like "hillbilly." Country folk lived on isolated farms away from the city; backwoods folks lived in remote areas, in the hill and hollers. To be from the backwoods was to be part of the wild. Where we lived, black folks were as much a part of the wild, living in a natural way on the earth, as white folks. All backwoods folks were poor by material standards; they knew how to make do. They were not wanting to tame the wildness, in themselves or nature. Living in the Kentucky hills was where I first learned the importance of being wild.

Ecological Cosmopolitanism

Later attending college on the West Coast I would come to associate the passion for freedom, for wildness I had experienced as a child, with anarchy, with the belief in the power of the individual to be self-determining. Writing about the connection between environments, nature, and creativity in the introduction to A Place in Space, [American poet] Gary Snyder states: "Ethics and aesthetics are deeply intertwined. Art, beauty and craft have always drawn on the self-organizing 'wild' side of language and mind. Human ideas of place and space, our contemporary focus on watersheds, become both models and metaphors. Our hope would be to see the interacting realms, learn where we are, and thereby move towards a style of planetary and ecological cosmopolitanism." Snyder calls this approach the "practice of the wild" urging us to live "in the self-disciplined elegance of 'wild' mind." By their own practice of living in harmony with nature, with simple abundance, Kentucky black folks who lived in the backwoods were deeply engaged with an ecological cosmopolitanism. They fished, hunted, raised chickens, planted what we would now call organic gardens, made homemade spirits, wine and whiskey, and grew flowers. Their religion was interior and private. Mama's mama, Baba, refused to attend church after someone had made fun of the clothes she was wearing. She reminded us that God could be worshipped every day anywhere. No matter that they lived according to Appalachian values, they did not talk about themselves as coming from Appalachia. They did not divide Kentucky into east and west. They saw themselves as renegades and rebels, folks who did not want to be hemmed in by rules and laws, folks that wanted to remain independent. Even when circumstances forced them out of the country into the city, they were still wanting to live free.

As there were individual black folks who explored the regions of this nation before slavery, the first black Appalachians being fully engaged with the Cherokee, the lives of most early black Kentuckians were shaped by a mixture of free sensibility and slave mentality. When slavery ended in Kentucky, life was hard for the vast majority of black people as white supremacy and racist domination did not end. But for those folks who managed to own land, especially land in isolated country sites or hills (sometimes inherited from white folks for whom they had worked for generations, or sometimes purchased), they were content to be self-defining and self-determining even if it meant living with less. No distinctions were made between those of us who dwelled in the hills of eastern or western Kentucky. Our relatives from eastern Kentucky did not talk about themselves as Appalachians, and in western Kentucky we did not use the term; even if one lived in the hills where the close neighbors were white and hillbilly, black people did not see themselves as united with these folks, even though our habits of being and ways of thinking were more like these strangers than those of other black folks who lived in the city—especially black folks who had money and city ways. In small cities and towns, the life of a black coal miner in western Kentucky was more similar to the life of an eastern counterpart than different. Just as the life of hillbilly black folks was the same whether they lived in the hills of eastern or western Kentucky.

Freedom and Integrity

In the Kentucky black subcultures, folks were united with our extended kin, and our identities were more defined by labels like country and backwoods. It was not until I went away to college that I was questioned about Appalachia, about hillbilly culture, and it was always assumed by these faraway outsiders that only poor white people lived in the backwoods and in the hills. No wonder then that black folks who cherish our past, the independence that characterized our backwoods ancestors, seek to recover and restore their history, their legacy. Early on in my life I learned from those Kentucky backwoods elders, the folks whom we might now label "Appalachian," a set of values rooted in the belief that above all else one must be self-determining. It is the foundation that is the root of my radical critical consciousness. Folks from the backwoods were certain about two things: that every human soul needed to be free and that the responsibility of being free required one to be a person of integrity, a person who lived in such a way that there would always be congruency between what we think, say, and do.

These ancestors had no interest in conforming to social norms and manners which made lying and cheating acceptable. More often than not they believed themselves to be above the law whenever the rules of so-called civilized culture made no sense. They farmed, fished, hunted and made their way in the world. Sentimental nostalgia does not call me to remember the worlds they invented. It is just a simple fact that without their early continued support for dissident thinking and living I would not have been able to hold my own in college and beyond when conformity promised to provide [me] with a sense of safety and greater regard. Their "Appalachian values," imprinted on my consciousness as core truths I must live by, provide and provided me with the tools I needed and need to survive whole in a postmodern world.

Living by those values, living with integrity, I am able to return to my native place, to an Appalachia that is no longer silent about its diversity or about the broad sweep of its influence. While I do not claim an identity as Appalachian, I do claim a solidarity, a sense of belonging, that makes me one with the Appalachian past of my ancestors, black, Native American, white, all "people of one blood" who made homeplace in isolated landscapes where they could invent themselves, where they could savor a taste of freedom.

For Further Discussion

1. How do London's own experiences in the Yukon gold rush inform the plot of *The Call of the Wild*? Consult viewpoints by Daniel Dyer, Charles Paul Freund, and James L. Haley to inform your answer.

2. Did *The Call of the Wild* and other works of London deserve to fall out of favor in the mid-twentieth century? Is *The Call of the Wild* on par with other great works of literature, or should it be classified as merely a young adult novel? See viewpoints by Daniel Dyer and Eric Miles Williamson to formulate your answer.

3. Is there a racist strain in *The Call of the Wild* in London's depiction, for example, of the Yeehats? Or is this criticism of London overblown? Consider viewpoints by Charles Paul Freund and Dan Davidson.

4. Are London's depictions of the animal world convincing and appropriate? Do they need to be, or is London's mythologizing of the natural world a valid strategy? See viewpoints by John Perry, S.K. Robisch, and Earle Labor and Jeanne Campbell Reesman to formulate your answer.

5. Is the ending of *The Call of the Wild*, in which Buck joins the wolf pack, a positive apotheosis into the natural world, or is it a sinister descent into pure, and perhaps malevolent, primitivism? See viewpoints by Richard Fusco, Raymond Benoit, Earle Labor and Jeanne Campbell Reesman, and Jacqueline Tavernier-Courbin.

6. Is "wildness" still a positive characteristic for a person in today's society? Can one be "wild" and still function as a productive member of adult society? See viewpoints by Jerry Adler, Suzanne Paola, and bell hooks to inform your answer.

7. Can wild animals and humans coexist in a civilized world? Are wild beasts still needed to remind us of the complexity of the modern world? Should a civilized society dedicate itself to ensuring the ongoing existence of wild animal life? Reference the viewpoint by the *Economist* to formulate your answer.

For Further Reading

Joseph Conrad, *Heart of Darkness*, 1899.

Charles Darwin, *Descent of Man*, 1871.

———, *On the Origin of Species*, 1859.

Roland Huntford, *Shackleton*. New York: Atheneum, 1986.

Rudyard Kipling, *The Jungle Book*, 1894.

Jon Krakauer, *Into the Wild*. New York: Villard Books, 1996.

———, *Into Thin Air: A Personal Account of the Mount Everest Disaster*. New York: Anchor Books/Doubleday, 1998.

Aldo Leopold, *A Sand County Almanac, and Sketches Here and There*. New York: Oxford University Press, 1987.

Jack London, *Martin Eden*. New York: Macmillan, 1909.

———, *The Sea-Wolf*. London: Heinemann, 1904.

———, *Son of the Wolf: Tales of the Far North*. New York: Grosset & Dunlap, 1900.

———, *White Fang*. London: Methuen, 1906.

Barry Lopez, *Arctic Dreams: Imagination and Desire in a Northern Landscape*. New York: Scribner, 1986.

———, *Of Wolves and Men*. New York: Scribner, 1978.

Desmond Morris, *The Naked Ape: A Zoologist's Study of the Human Animal*. London: Cape, 1967.

———, *Dogwatching*. New York: Crown Publishers, 1986.

Friedrich Wilhelm Nietzsche, *Thus Spoke Zarathustra*, 1883.

Robert W. Service, *The Spell of the Yukon and Other Verses*. New York: Barse & Hopkins, 1907.

Gary Snyder, *The Practice of the Wild*. San Francisco, CA: North Point Press, 1990.

Henry David Thoreau, *Walden*, 1854.

Bibliography

Books

Cass Adams, ed.	*The Soul Unearthed: Celebrating Wildness and Personal Renewal Through Nature*. New York: Jeremy P. Tarcher/Putnam, 1996.
Bruce T. Batchelor	*Nine Dog Winter*. Victoria, BC: Agio Publishing House, 2008.
Lawrence I. Berkove, ed.	*Jack London*. Pasadena, CA: Salem Press, 2012.
Pierre Berton	*The Klondike Fever: The Life and Death of the Last Great Gold Rush*. New York: Alfred A. Knopf, 1959.
Katie De Koster, ed.	*Readings on The Call of the Wild*. San Diego, CA: Greenhaven Press, 1999.
E.L. Doctorow	*Jack London, Hemingway, and the Constitution: Selected Essays, 1977–1992*. New York: Random House, 1993.
John Firth	*River Time: Racing the Ghosts of the Klondike Rush*. Edmonton: NeWest Press, 2004.
Joan D. Hedrick	*Solitary Comrade, Jack London and His Work*. Chapel Hill: University of North Carolina Press, 1982.
Alex Kershaw	*Jack London: A Life*. New York: St. Martin's Press, 1998.

Eugene Kinkead   *Wildness Is All Around Us: Notes of an Urban Naturalist.* New York: Dutton, 1978.

Jack London   *The Call of the Wild: A Casebook with Text Background Sources, Reviews, Critical Essays and Bibliography.* Ed. Earl J. Wilcox. Chicago: Nelson-Hall, 1980.

Jack London   *The Call of the Wild: Complete Text with Introduction, Historical Contexts, Critical Essays.* Eds. Earl J. Wilcox and Elizabeth H. Wilcox. Boston, MA: Houghton Mifflin, 2004.

Jack London   *The Call of the Wild, White Fang, and Other Stories.* Ed. Andrew Sinclair. New York: Penguin Books, 1981, pp. 7–16.

Joan London   *Jack London and His Times: An Unconventional Biography.* Seattle: University of Washington Press, 1968.

James Lundquist   *Jack London, Adventures, Ideas, and Fiction.* New York: Ungar, 1987.

Susan M. Nuernberg   *The Critical Response to Jack London.* Westport, CT: Greenwood Press, 1995.

Richard O'Connor   *Jack London: A Biography.* Boston, MA: Little, Brown and Company, 1964.

Mary E. Papke — *Twisted from the Ordinary: Essays on American Literary Naturalism.* Knoxville: University of Tennessee Press, 2003.

Jeanne Campbell Reesman — *Critical Companion to Jack London: A Literary Reference to His Life and Work.* New York: Facts on File, 2011.

Gay Salisbury and Laney Salisbury — *The Cruelest Miles: The Heroic Story of Dogs and Men in a Race Against an Epidemic.* New York: W.W. Norton & Co, 2003.

Donna Seaman — *In Our Nature: Stories of Wildness.* New York: Dorling Kindersley, 2000.

Bill Sherwonit — *Living with Wildness: An Alaskan Odyssey.* Fairbanks: University of Alaska Press, 2008.

Andrew Sinclair — *Jack: A Biography of Jack London.* New York: Harper & Row, 1977.

Jacqueline Tavernier-Courbin — *Critical Essays on Jack London.* Boston, MA: G.K. Hall, 1983.

Charles Child Walcutt — *Jack London.* Minneapolis: University of Minnesota Press, 1966.

Laura Waterman and Guy Waterman — *Wilderness Ethics: Preserving the Spirit of Wildness.* Woodstock, VT: Countryman Press, 1993.

Periodicals

Jonathan Auerbach — "'Congested Mails': Buck and Jack's 'Call,'" *American Literature*, vol. 67, no. 1, March 1995.

Sam S. Baskett   "Jack London's Heart of Darkness," *American Quarterly*, vol. 10, no. 1, Spring 1958.

Pierre Berton   "Gold Rush Writing," *Canadian Literature*, 1960.

Lawrence Clayton   "The Ghost Dog, a Motif in *The Call of the Wild*," *Jack London Newsletter*, vol. 5, September–December 1972.

Frank Clifford   "Wild in the Yukon—Photographer Jannik Schou Braves Northern Yukon Forests to Document a Pristine Wilderness That Environmentalists Say Is Threatened by Industry," *Smithsonian*, vol. 37, no. 4, 2006.

William Cronon   "The Trouble with Wilderness; Or, Getting Back to the Wrong Nature," *Environmental History*, vol. 1, no. 1, January 1996.

Daniel Dyer   "Answering the Call of the Wild," *English Journal*, vol. 77, no. 4, 1988.

Sophie Elmhirst   "Every Now and Then Something Pops Out of the Forest to Remind Us About the Wildness," *New Statesman*, May 10, 2013.

Andrew Flink   "*Call of the Wild*—Jack London's Catharsis," *Jack London Newsletter*, vol. 11, January–April 1978.

Andrew Flink   "*Call of the Wild*—Parental Metaphor," *Jack London Newsletter*, vol. 7, May–August 1974.

Charles Frey — "Contradiction in *The Call of the Wild*," *Jack London Newsletter*, vol. 12, January–December 1979.

Caroline Hanssen — "'You Were Right, Old Hoss; You Were Right': Jack London in Jon Krakauer's *Into the Wild*," *American Literary Realism*, vol. 43, no. 3, Spring 2011.

Michael Kumin — "*The Call of the Wild*: London's Seven Stages of Allegory," *Jack London Newsletter*, vol. 21, January–December 1988.

Earle Labor — "Jack London's Mondo Cane: *The Call of the Wild* and *White Fang*," *Jack London Newsletter*, vol. 1, July–December 1967.

Carolyn Lott and Stephanie Wasta — "Lessons Learned from Hobbs, London, and the Yukon Gold Rush," *Alan Review*, vol. 35, no. 2, Winter 2008.

Mario Maffi — "The Law of Life: Jack London and the Dialectic of Nature," *Jack London Newsletter*, vol. 12, January–December 1979.

Scott Malcomson — "The Inevitable White Man: Jack London's Endless Journey," *Voice Literary Supplement*, vol. 1, February 1994.

Susan M. Nuernberg	"'Give Us Howling and Naked Savagery': Jack London and *The Call of the Wild*," *English Journal*, vol. 85, no. 5, September 1996.
Ellen Paneok	"Arctic Journeys: Flying Amid the Raw Wildness and Delicate Beauty of Alaska," *Defense Transportation Journal*, December 2011.
Jonah Raskin	"Calls of the Wild on the Page and Screen: From Jack London and Gary Snyder to Jon Krakauer and Sean Penn," *American Literary Realism*, vol. 43, no. 3, Spring 2011.
A. Paul Reed	"Running with the Pack: Jack London's *The Call of the Wild* and Jesse Stuart's *Mongrel Mettle*," *Jack London Newsletter*, vol. 18, September–December 1985.
Abraham Rothberg	"Land Dogs and Sea Wolves: A Jack London Dilemma," *Massachusetts Review*, vol. 21, no. 3, Fall 1980.
Earl J. Wilcox	"Jack London's Naturalism: The Example of *The Call of the Wild*," *Jack London Newsletter*, vol. 2, September–December 1969.
T. Williams	"Jack London: The Call of the Wild," *Studies in Short Fiction*, vol. 33, no. 3, 1996.

Index

A

Absolutist thinking and racism, 39–40

The Abysmal Brute (London), 10–11

Adams, Nick (Hemingway character), 16

Adaptability
Buck, 11, 78, 91, 94, 96
test of heroic quest, 78
Van Weyden, Humphrey *(The Sea Wolf)*, 10, 124
wolves, 160

Adventure stage of heroic quest, 76, 83

The Adventures of Huckleberry Finn (Twain), 16, 69, 74, 109, 111–112

The Aegis (magazine), 27, 49

Aesop's fables, 103, 107, 108, 126

Aesthetics
critical reception, 57
ecological cosmopolitanism, 173
environmentalism, 38

African American freedom and wildness, 172–176

Ahab *(Moby-Dick)*, 119, 144–145

Alaska and wolves, 156

Alaskan husky. *See* Huskies

Alcohol, 23, 58

Alexander, Sidney, 128

The Alhambra (Irving), 26

Alienation
London's popularity, 54–62
technology, 38, 40

All-terrain vehicles, 153

American dream and wildness, 9, 70, 112

Amorality. *See* Morality

Ancestral knowledge and traits. *See* Atavism

Anderson, Sherwood, 70

Animals
fables/parables, 102–108
parallels with humans, 12, 15, 60–61, 100–101, 122–129
unrealistic depictions, 105, 122–129, 130, 134
See also Buck *(The Call of the Wild)*; Spitz *(The Call of the Wild)*; Wolves

"The Apostate" (London), 105–106

Apotheosis, 76, 80, 83–84, 110, 120, 137

Appalachia, 172–176

Archetypes and devolution, 98–101

Argentina, 152–153

Around-the-world sailing, 9–10, 30–32

Artists
Buck as, 14, 80
fable and parable form, 103
Van Weyden, Humphrey *(The Sea Wolf)*, 145

Aryan movement, 40

Atavism
anti-capitalism, 87, 91–93
"Bâtard" (London), 134

Buck's survival and development, 11–15, 70, 71, 96–98, 110, 134, 141
depravity and decay, 124
epigraph to *The Call of the Wild,* 11, 85
fable/parable, 106
"Husky: The Wolf-Dog of the North" (London), 131
killing instinct, 97–98
naturalism, 12, 138
rebirth stage of heroic quest, 82
strength, 106
violence, 138
White Fang (London), 106
whiteness, 118
wolf myths, 137
See also Devolution; Primitivism
"Atavism" (O'Hara), 11, 85
Atlantic Monthly, 54
Audubon, John James, 157
Auerbach, Jonathan, 87
Austen, Jane, 60
Australia, 32
Austria and wolves, 160
Autodidactism, 14, 23, 57

B

Backpacking, decline, 151
Backwoods living and freedom, 172–176
Bad girls, 166–171
Baker, Kim, 162, 164
"Bâtard" (London), 75–76, 125, 130–139
Bears, 98, 147, 160, 161
Beatings
devolution, 95
dog breaker, 77–78, 86, 95, 99
Hal, 81
heroic quest, 77–78, 81
White Fang (London), 143
Beauty *(White Fang),* 107
Beaver, Gary *(White Fang),* 143
Beavers, 161
Before Adam (London), 91
Belgium, and wolves, 156, 160
Bellew, Smoke (fictional character), 29, 118
Bennett Lake, 50
Benoit, Raymond, 69–74
Berkeley Advance (newspaper), 123
Bern Convention of 1979, 159–160
"Big Two-Hearted River" (Hemingway), 16, 71
Bison, 161
Black bear, 98
"Black" Burton (*The Call of the Wild*), 100
Blood-and-soil movements, 40
Bly, Robert, 71
Boar, 156, 157
Boisguilbert, Pierre de, 163
Boitani, Luigi, 164–165
Bond, Hiram G., 28
Bond, Louis, 28
Bond, Marshall, 28
Bonner, Neil ("The Story of Jees Uck"), 126
Bookman (magazine), 123
Boston, MA, 156
Bounties, wolves, 156
Boxing, 10–11
Bramwell, Anna, 40
Brewster, Maud (*The Sea-Wolf*), 124
Brown bears, 160

"Brown Wolf" (London), 128
Browning, Dominique, 152–153
Buck (*The Call of the Wild*), 72, 79, 90, 119
 apotheosis, 76, 80, 83–84, 110, 120, 137
 atavism, 11–15, 70, 71, 96–98, 110, 134, 141
 Campbell's heroic quest, 75–84, 110
 capitalism, 85–93
 devolution, 12–13, 16, 63–68, 94–101
 fable/parable, 106
 ghost dog myth, 16, 68, 75, 83–84, 120–121
 human traits, 11–12, 15, 76–84
 identification with London, 14
 individualism quest, 140–142
 inspiration for, 28
 pastoralism, 69–74
 rejection of civilization, 11–16, 63–68, 69–74, 76, 85–93, 94–101, 109–121
 Rousseau's development of man, 63–68
 syntactical style, 69, 74
 whiteness, 120–121
 work, 112–115
Buffalo, NY, 49
Bullock, Thomas, 156
Burning Daylight (London), 128
Burroughs, Edgar Rice, 39

C

California
 Bond ranch, 28
 Glen Ellen ranch, 32–33, 129
 Jack London State Historic Park, 33

Oakland, 23, 25–26, 27, 47–48, 49
California Fish Patrol, 26, 48
The Call of the Wild (London), 72, 79, 90, 119
 anti-capitalism, 56, 85–93
 autobiographical elements, 14, 23
 Campbell's stages of heroic quest, 75–84, 110
 critical reception, 56, 105, 122–123, 123, 125–126
 devolution, 11–16, 63–68, 94–101
 Dyer edition, 138–139
 fable/parable form, 102–108
 individualism, 111, 140–148
 insights from "Husky: The Wolf-Dog of the North" (London), 130–139
 inspiration, 28
 London on, 75–76
 pastoralism, 69–74
 Rousseau's development of man, 63–68
 society vs. wildness, 109–121
 unrealistic depiction of animals, 105, 122–129, 130, 134
 See also Civilization; Wildness
"Call to adventure stage," heroic quests, 76, 83
Campbell, Donna M., 12
Campbell, Joseph, 75–84, 110
Camping, 151, *152*
Canada
 allegations of London's racism, 35, 37, 41, 42
 wolves, 160
 Yukon gold rush, 9, 14, 23, 27–29, 46–52, *51*
Cannery work, 47

Cannibalism
  capitalism, 87
  Curly, 78, 87, 95
  husky breed, 132
  Spitz, 13
Capitalism, rejection
  Buck's escape to wildness,
    85–93
  critical reception, 56
  hobos, 49
  London's writings and politi-
    cal activities, 37–38, 52
  The People of the Abyss
    (London), 45
  racism, 42, 45
Caras, Roger A., 128
Cattle wolf kills, 162
Caveman dream, 15, 122–123
Chaney, John. *See* London, Jack
Chaney, William, 25, 46, 47
Chapron, Guillaume, 161
Charles (*The Call of the Wild*)
  capitalism, 88–89
  incompetence, 71–74, 81, 101,
    114
  morality, 107
  syntactical style, 69, 73–74
  work ethic, 112–113, 114
Chase, Richard, 76–77
Cheechakoes
  capitalism, 88–89
  incompetence, 67, 71–74, 81,
    101, 114
  London's Yukon trip, 50
  morality, 107
  racism, 45
  syntactical style, 69, 73–74
  work ethic, 112–113, 114
Cherokee tribe, 174
Chilkoot Pass, 50
"The Chinago" (London), 105

Chippewa tribe, 162
Civilization
  The Abysmal Brute (London),
    10–11
  Buck's metamorphosis, 11–16,
    63–68, 69–74, 76, 85–93,
    94–101, 109–121
  capitalism, 85–93
  devolution, 12–13, 16, 60–61,
    63–68, 94–101, 123–124
  hooks, bell, 172–176
  individualism, 140–148
  Martin Eden (London), 10
  Moby-Dick (Melville), 109,
    118–120
  naturalism, 12, 94
  Nick Adams stories
    (Hemingway), 16
  pastoralism, 69–74
  racism, 34–41
  Rousseau's stages of man's
    development, 63–68
  The Sea Wolf (London), 10
  "The Somnambulists"
    (London), 60–61, 124
  Twain, Mark, 16, 61, 69, 74,
    109, 111–112
  White Fang (London), 106–
    108, 135
  vs. wildness, 109–121
Clark, Jamie Rappaport, 162
Coal shoveling employment, 23,
  48, 52
Communism. *See* Socialism
The Communist Manifesto (Marx),
  37
Competition
  among sled dogs, 84, 88
  parable, 107
  wolves vs. humans, 159
  writing, 26, 48
  See also Capitalism, rejection

Conrad, Joseph, 113
Conservation
    boar and deer, 157
    Leopold, Aldo, 157–159
    Roosevelt, Theodore, 39
    wolves, 154–165
Cooper, James Fenimore, 61
Corliss, Vance (*A Daughter of the Snows*), 44, 113
Cotton, John, 71
Country living and freedom, 172–176
Coxey, Jacob, 24
Coxey's Industrial Army, 24
Crane, Stephen, 12, 25
Critical reception
    The Call of the Wild, 56, 105, 122–123, 125–126
    disinterest in London, 54–62, 102–103
    unrealism, 105, 122–129, 130, 134
    White Fang (London), 56, 105
Crucifixion imagery, 81
The Cruise of the Dazzler (London), 26
The Cruise of the Snark (London), 32
"A Curious Fragment" (London), 37
Curly (*The Call of the Wild*), 78, 85, 86–87, 95

D

Darwin, Charles, 28
Darwinism
    vs. anti-capitalism, 86, 87, 88, 92
    fight with Spitz, 13–15

London, 69, 133
    See also Devolution
A Daughter of the Snows (London)
    inspiration, 29
    racism, 44, 45
    wildness vs. society, 110
    work, 113
Dave (*The Call of the Wild*), 96, 99, 114
Davidson, Dan, 42–45
Dawson City, YT, 28, 51, *51*
Dead Horse Gulch, 50
Deane, Paul, 140–148
Death
    Buck's symbolic, 80–81
    Charles, Hal, and Mercedes, 81, 101
    Curly, 78, 85, 86–87, 95
    fear, 60, 92
    London, Jack, 23, 33
    Thornton, John, 15–16, 67, 83, 91, 99, 107, 110
Deer, 156, 157
Defenders of Wildlife, 162
Demon imagery
    "Bâtard" (London), 135
    whiteness, 119
Denmark and wolves, 156
Departure stage of heroic quest, 76
Destiny
    heroic quest, 82, 83
    manifest destiny, 159
    myth, 78
    power, 102, 108
    racial, 38
Determinism, 12, 135, 136, 137
Devolution
    Buck, 12–13, 16, 63–68, 94–101
    depravity, 123–124

Rousseau's stages of man's development, 63–68

"The Somnambulists" (London), 60–61, 124

See also Atavism; Primitivism

Discourse on Inequality (Rousseau), 64–65

Dog breaker (*The Call of the Wild*)

    capitalism, 86

    devolution, 95

    initiation stage of heroic quest, 77–78

    objectivity of style, 99

Dog sled team, *79*

    competition, 84, 88

    Curly's death, 78, 85, 86–87, 95

    family, 66–67

    song, 78–80, 114

    See also Spitz (*The Call of the Wild*)

Dogs

    "Husky: The Wolf-Dog of the North" (London), 130–139

    unrealistic depictions, 122–129, 130, 134

    wolf kills, 163

    See also Buck (*The Call of the Wild*); Dog sled team; Spitz (*The Call of the Wild*)

Dream imagery, caveman, 15, 122–123

Dreiser, Theodore, 25

Drug use and wildness, 166–168

Duck hunting, decline, 151

Dyea, AK, 28, 50

Dyer, Daniel, 23–33, 138–139

E

Eating

    cannibalism, 13, 78, 87, 95, 132

    human fighting over food, 14

    stealing food, 12, 78, 87–88, 96, 133

Ecological cosmopolitanism, 173

Ecstasy, 14, 80, 113

Eden imagery in *The Abysmal Brute* (London), 10–11

Edgar, King of England, 155

Education

    Buck, 11, 78, 87, 94–96, 141

    London, Jack, 25, 27, 46, 49

    Martin Eden (London), 147

    racism, 44

    The Sea Wolf (London), 146–147

    wild side, 169

Edward I, King of England, 155

Eliot, T.S., 55

Elk, 161

"The End of the Story" (London), 124

Endangered Species Act (1973), 159

England and wolves, 155

Environment and naturalism, 12, 94, 98

Environmentalism

    aesthetics, 38

    conservation, 39, 154–165

    Leopold, Aldo, 157–159, *158*

    racism, 35–41

Equal Rights Amendment, 169

Erie County Penitentiary (NY), 24

Escape

    The Adventures of Huckleberry Finn (Twain), 112

Buck's escape from capitalism, 85–93
Ethics. *See* Morality
Europe
bears, 160
blood-and-soil movements, 40
wolves, 137–138, 154–165
Evil
"Bâtard" (London), 130, 135
ghost dog, 120
human, 132
White Fang (London), 130, 135
wolves, 157
Excelsior (ship), 27, 46, 49
Existentialism, 137

F

Fables
form in *The Call of the Wild*, 102–108
wolves, 126
Fairness, 78, 87, 95, 96
Fame, 23, 55, 136
Family
London's marriages and family, 23, 30, 58
stage of man's development, 63, 64, 65
types in *The Call of the Wild*, 64, 65–68
Farmers and wolf policy, 154, 162–164
Fascism, 34, 37, 40
Father imagery
Buck, 16, 120
Spitz, 118, 119
Thornton, John, 118
Faulkner, William, 71

Fear
death, 60, 92
humans, 127–128, 143, 155
Fenris myth, 137
50-Mile River, 50
Fighting
alternative to working, 114
anti-capitalism, 85, 86, 88
Charles, Hal, and Mercedes, 73
Darwinism, 13–15
devolution, 97–98
husky breed, 132
individualism and ritual, 118, 119, 141
London, Jack, 23
survival and morality, 14, 123
Films
disinterest in wilderness, 151
novelization by London, 24
Finland and wolves, 160, 164
Finn, Huck (*The Adventures of Huckleberry Finn*), 16, 109, 111–112
Fire at "Wolf House," 23, 32–33
First Nations peoples. *See* Native Americans
Fish Patrol, CA, 26, 48
Fisher, Peter S., 38
Fishing, decline, 151
Food. *See* Eating
France
bears, 160
wolves, 156, 159, 160, 162–163, 164–165
Francois (*The Call of the Wild*), 86, 112, 114, 115, 116
Franklin, H. Bruce, 37, 38
Free will and naturalism, 12

Freedom
American dream and wild-
ness, 9
Buck, 15–16, 67
individualism, 140–148
Moby-Dick (Melville), 144–145
The Sea-Wolf (London), 144–
145
White Fang (London), 142
wildness and integrity, 172–
176
Freud, Sigmund, 119
Freund, Charles Paul, 34–41
'Frisco Kid persona, 23, 24–25
Fusco, Richard, 63–68

G

Gaia thesis, 40
Gasoline prices and disinterest in
wilderness, 151
Geismar, Maxwell, 76
Geography
London's Yukon trip, 50–51
realism in London's works, 25
George (*Of Mice and Men*), 55
Germany
London's popularity and rac-
ism, 38
mysticism, 38, 40
wolves, 156, 160
The Ghost (fictional ship). *See The
Sea Wolf* (London)
Ghost dog
atavism, 11
myth, 16, 68, 75, 83–84, 120–
121
whiteness, 118, 120–121
Los Glaciares National Park
(Argentina), 152–153
Glen Ellen, CA, 32–33, 129

Glendon, Pat (*The Abysmal Brute*),
10–11
Gloersen, Gunnar, 163
The God of His Fathers (London),
101, 128
Gold rush, London's activities, 9,
14, 23, 27–29, 46–52, *51*
Graham, Stephen, 129
Grant, Madison, 39
Grief, 118
Grizzly bears, 160, 161
Guth, Marie-Odile, 159

H

Habitat
legislation, 160, 164
wolves, 156–157
Habitats Directive of 1992, 160,
164
Hal (*The Call of the Wild*)
capitalism, 88–89
incompetence, 71–74, 81, 101,
114
morality, 107
syntactical style, 69, 73–74
work ethic, 112–113, 114
Haley, James L., 14, 46–52
Hamsun, Knut, 35, 38
Hans (*The Call of the Wild*), 73
Harper's (magazine), 130
Hawaii, 10, 32
Health, London's, 9, 23, 32, 33, 52
Heart failure, 33
Heart of Darkness (Conrad), 113
Hearts of Three (London), 128
Hemingway, Ernest, 16, 57, 71, 74
Henry (*White Fang*), 127
Heredity
mythical style, 98–101

naturalism, 12, 94, 96–97
  See also Atavism
The Hero with a Thousand Faces
  (Campbell), 83
Heroism
  Buck and Campbell's stages of
    heroic quest, 75–84, 110
  Buck as American hero, 70, 71
  Hemingway hero, 74
  Larsen, Wolf (*The Sea-Wolf*),
    145
  strength, 102, 105
  Thornton, John (*The Call of
    the Wild*), 101
Hesse, Hermann, 137–138
The Hidden Life of Dogs
  (Thomas), 138
Hillbillies. *See* Appalachia
Hobos, 9, 23, 24–25, 48–49
Hoffman, Frederick J., 124
hooks, bell, 172–176
Horses, 50, 120
*The House of Pride and Other
  Tales of Hawaii* (London), 32
Humans
  Buck as stand-in, 11–12, 15,
    76–84
  caveman dream, 15, 122–123
  cruelty, 77–78, 95, 135, 136,
    138, 143
  evil, 132
  fear of, 127–128, 143, 155
  fighting over food, 14
  incompetence, 67, 71–74, 81,
    101, 114
  morality, 100–101, 107–108
  parallels with animals, 12, 15,
    60–61, 100–101, 122–129
  Rousseau's stages of man's
    development, 63–68
  work ethic, 112–113

Hunting
  alternative to working, 114–
    115
  conservation, 39
  decline, 151
  ecstasy, 113
  moose, 163
  rabbit, 97, 118, 119
  seal, 9, 10, 23, 26, 48
  wolves, 154, 155–158, 164–165
Huskies, 130–139
  See also Buck (*The Call of the
    Wild*); Dog sled team
"Husky: The Wolf-Dog of the
  North" (London), 130–139
Huxley, Thomas, 13

I

Idaho and wolves, 160
Idealism, conflict with naturalism,
  111
Idwal, King of Wales, 155
Immortality
  ghost dog, 83
  "The White Silence"
    (London), 60
Imprisonment, 9, 23, 49
"In a Far Country" (London), 81,
  101, 125
In Our Time (Hemingway), 71
Incompetence and survival, 67,
  71–74, 81, 101, 114
Independence. *See* Freedom
Indifference of nature, 54, 61, 136
Individualism
  conflict with naturalism, 111
  freedom and integrity in wild-
    ness, 173–174
  paradox of quest, 140–148
Individuation, 75, 84, 110

Industrialization
  racism, 35–37
  rejection, 69–74
  See also Civilization
Initiation stage of heroic quest, 75, 76, 77–80, 110
Integrity and wildness, 172–176
Internet and disinterest in wilderness, 150, 151
Ipswich, MA, 156
The Iron Heel (London), 37, 105, 124, 136
Iroquois White Dog sacrifice, 119
Irving, Washington, 26
Ishmael *(Moby-Dick)*, 109, 119
Isolation
  freedom in solitude, 67
  London's popularity, 54, 58–62
  loneliness, 148
Italy and wolves, 156, 160–161

J

Jack London: A Life (Kershaw), 58
Jack London State Historic Park (CA), 33
Jail, 9, 23, 49
James, Henry, 25, 60
Janitorial work, 49
Japan, 9, 26, 56–57
Jim *(The Adventures of Huckleberry Finn)*, 112
John Barleycorn (London), 106, 118
Josselyn, John, 156
Jouffrey, Joseph, 162–163
Journalism, 23, 26, 48
Judge Miller *(The Call of the Wild)*, 11, 66, 113, 115

Jung, Carl, 13, 33, 84, 105, 135
The Jungle Book (Kipling), 104, 105

K

Kaczynski, Ted, 40
Kazin, Alfred, 109
Kennicott, Carol *(Main Street)*, 70
Kent State University, 167
Kentucky country and backwoods, 172–176
Kershaw, Alex, 58
Kiche *(White Fang)*, 107
Kidney failure, 33
Killing
  alternative to working, 114–115
  Buck's willingness, 88, 97–99
  wolves, 126–127, 136, 137
  Yeehats, 15, 67, 68, 83, 91, 92, 99
  See also Death; Hunting
Kingman, Russ, 134
Kipling, Rudyard, 104, 105
Kittredge, Charmian, 9–10, 30–32, *31*, 58
Klondike gold rush, London's activities, 9, 14, 23, 27–29, 46–52, *51*
Klondike Sun (newspaper), 42–45
Koskoosh ("The Law of Life"), 126–127, 136
Krebs ("Soldier's Home"), 74
Kumin, Michael, 87, 92
Kwanlin Dun tribe, 35

L

Laberge Lake, 51
Labiskwee ("Wonder of Woman"),
118
Labor
Buck's escape from capitalism,
85–93
movement, 24, 47
Labor, Earle, 10, 75–84, 105, 108,
110, 119
Larsen, Wolf (*The Sea Wolf*), 10,
14, 144–147, 148
Laundry work, 23, 27, 49
"The Law of Life" (London), 126–
127, 136
Laws and morality, 175
Leadership, Buck's
anti-capitalism, 85, 86, 88
Campbell's stages of heroic
quest, 75, 78, 83–84
Darwinism, 13–15
devolution and anarchy, 68,
97–98, 114–115, 141
family dynamics, 66–67
Judge Miller's farm, 11
quest for individualism, 141
Rousseau's stages of development, 64, 66, 67, 68
sled dog team, 13–15, 66–67,
78, 85, 86, 88, 114–115, 141
unrealism, 130, 134
wolf pack, 64, 67, 68, 83–84,
120, 130, 134
Leadership in *White Fang*
(London), 143–144
Learning. *See* Education; Unlearning
Lenin, Vladimir, 37
Leopold, Aldo, 157–159, *158*
Lewis, Sinclair, 70

"Li Wan, the Fair" (London), 124
Liberals and wolf policy, 154, 163
Libido, 84
Lindeman Lake, 50
The Little Lady of the Big House
(London), 33
The Log of the Snark (Kittredge),
32
London, Becky, 30
London, Charmian. *See* Kittredge,
Charmian
London, Flora. *See* Wellman, Flora
London, Jack, *31, 36, 59*
biography, 23–33, 58
on *The Call of the Wild*, 75–76
childhood, 25–26
critical reception, 54–62, 102–
103, 105, 122–129, 130, 134
death, 23, 33
education, 25, 27, 46, 49
fable/parable form, 102–108
fame, 23, 55, 136
'Frisco Kid persona, 23, 24–25
health, 9, 23, 32, 33, 52
identification with Buck, 14
imprisonment, 9, 23, 49
jobs, 9, 23, 27, 46, 47–48
marriages and family, 23, 30,
58
political activities, 23, 37–38
racism, 34–41, 42–45, 54–62,
92
travels, 9–10, 14, 23, 24–25,
27–29, 30–32, 46–52
London, Joan, 30, 76
London, John, 26
Lopez, Barry, 126, 138
Los Glaciares National Park
(Argentina), 152–153
Love
Judge Miller, 66, 115

Thornton, John, 67, 100, 107, 115, 116, 142

White Fang (London), 107, 135

wolf pack, 68

"Love of Life" (London), 127

Lovejoy, Arthur O., 64–65

Lucifer (*Paradise Lost*), 145

Lunden, John. *See* London, Jack

Lynx, 105, 160

M

Machismo, 57, 126, 128

Maddern, Bessie May, 30

Main Street (Lewis), 70

Malemute Kid (*The God of His Fathers*), 101

Manifest destiny, 159

Marlow, Charles (*Heart of Darkness*), 113

Marriages and divorces, 23, 30, 58

Marsh Lake, 50

Martin Eden (London)
autobiographical elements, 10, 27
disinterest, 136
fable/parable form, 106
individualism, 140, 147–148
suicide, 10, 140, 148

Marx, Karl, 37, 133

Mary (queen of Scotland), 155

Masculinity. *See* Machismo

Mason, Bill, 127–128

Massachusetts and wolves, 156

McGeshick, Chris, 162

Mech, L. David, 127, 164

Melville, Herman, 109, 116, 118–120, 144–145

Mercedes (*The Call of the Wild*)
capitalism, 88–89

incompetence, 71–74, 81, 101, 114
morality, 107
syntactical style, 69, 73–74
work ethic, 112–113, 114

Mercy, 13, 96, 98

Metamorphosis
Campbell's stages of heroic quest, 75, 77, 78
devolution and amorality, 94

Metzger, Tom, 40

Michael, Brother of Jerry (London), 125–126

Mill work, 48

Miller, Judge (*The Call of the Wild*), 11, 66, 113, 115

Milton, John, 145

Minnesota and wolves, 156

Missouri, 24

Moby-Dick (Melville), 109, 116, 118–120, 144–145

Montana and wolves, 162

Moose
hunting in Sweden, 163
imagery, 98–99

Morality
amorality of nature, 135
"Bâtard" (London), 125
characterization, 107
devolution, 94, 96, 100–101
ecological cosmopolitanism, 173
fables/parables, 103, 104
humans, 100–101, 107–108
"In a Far Country" (London), 101
laws, 175
naturalism, 99
survival, 14, 94, 123, 124–125, 133
wildness and racism, 34, 40

wolves, 130, 136
See also Stealing
Morris, Desmond, 138
Morse, Ruth (Martin Eden), 147
Mowat, Farley, 127
Muir, John, 38, 40
Mysticism, Nazi, 38, 40
Myth
    The Adventures of Huckleberry
        Finn (Twain), 112
    ancestral, 97, 98–101
    Campbell's heroic quest, 75–
        84, 110
    destiny, 78
    Fenris, 137
    ghost dog, 16, 68, 75, 83–84,
        120–121
    "Husky: The Wolf-Dog of the
        North" (London), 132
    primordial strength, 105, 110
    The Sea Wolf (London), 136
    unconscious and Carl Jung,
        33, 84
    wolves, 137, 162

N

Nash, Roderick, 39
National parks. See Parks
Native Americans
    Appalachia, 174, 176
    London's portrayals, 45
    London's racism, 35, 43
    White Dog sacrifice, 119
    wolf mythology, 162
    See also Yeehats
Natural selection, 13–14
    See also Darwinism
Naturalism
    atavism, 12, 138
    Buck's regression, 69–74

conflict with individuation,
    111
devolution, 94–101
heroic quest, 77
racism, 34–41
realism, 12, 25
The Sea Wolf (London), 124
Nature
    amorality, 135
    Eden imagery in The Abysmal
        Brute (London), 10–11
    indifference, 54, 61, 136
    vs. man, 12
    vs. nurture, 130, 135–136
Nature Conservancy, 151
'Nature faker,' 105, 125–126
Nazism, 38, 44
Netherlands and wolves, 154–155,
    160
Never Cry Wolf (Mowat), 127
New Mexico and wolves, 158
New York, 9, 23, 24, 49
Niagara Falls, NY, 9, 23, 24, 49
Nick Adams stories (Hemingway),
    16
Nietzsche, Friedrich, 69, 102, 133,
    137
Nobility
    Thornton, John, 73
    wildness and racism, 34, 39
Nordicism. See Racism
Norris, Frank, 12, 25, 111
Norway and wolves, 156
Novick, Michael, 40
Nuernberg, Susan, 42–45

O

Oakland, CA, 23, 25–26, 27, 47–
    48, 49
Oakland High School, 27, 49

"An Odyssey of the North"
(London), 54, 56
Of Mice and Men (Steinbeck), 55
Of Wolves and Men (Lopez), 126
O'Hara, John Myers, 11, 85
On the Origin of Species (Darwin),
28
Outdoor activities, decline, 151
Overland Monthly, 54
Ownership
    capitalism, 85, 86, 88–91
    violence, 95
Oyster piracy, 9, 23, 26, 47

P

Pacific travels, 9, 32
Pain
    devolution and callousness, 96
    objective style, 99
    song of the huskies, 78–80
Panic of 1893, 47
Paola, Suzanne, 166–171
Parable in *The Call of the Wild*,
102–108
Paradise Lost (Milton), 145
Parks
    decline in interest, 151
    Jack London State Historic
    Park, 33
    overcrowding, 150, 152
    wolves, 159, 160, 161, 163
    Yellowstone National Park,
    152, 159, 160, 161
The Passing of the Great Race
(Grant), 39
Past, Buck's link. *See* Atavism
Pastoralism, 69–74
Patricide, 118, 119
The People of the Abyss (London),
45, 124

Pergams, Oliver, 151–153
Perrault (*The Call of the Wild*), 86,
112, 114, 115, 116
Perry, John, 122–129
Pete (*The Call of the Wild*), 73
Piracy, oyster, 9, 23, 26, 47
Pizer, Donald, 102–108
A Place in Space (Snyder), 173
Point of view, 11
Poland and wolves, 160
Politics
    critical reception, 54
    London's activities, 23, 37–38
    wolf policy, 154–165
Prentiss, Jennie, 26
Primitivism
    *The Adventures of Huckleberry
    Finn* (Twain), 112
    anti-capitalism, 91–93
    caveman dream, 15, 122–123
    critical reception, 122–124
    cruelty and violence, 138
    individuation, 110
    Moby-Dick (Melville), 109
    racism, 34, 38
    romanticism, 110
    Rousseau's development of
    man, 63–68
    The Sea-Wolf (London), 144
    See also Atavism; Devolution
Prison, 9, 23, 49
Protection. *See* Conservation
Protests
    anti-war, 167
    anti-wolf, 163
    labor and unemployment, 24,
    47
    wildness and, 169–170

Q

Quests
Campbell's heroic, 75–84, 110
paradox of individualism,
140–148

R

Rabbit imagery
"The End of the Story"
(London), 124
killing instincts, 97
whiteness, 118, 119
Racism
A Daughter of the Snows
(London), 44, 45
Kentucky, 174
London was not racist, 42–45
London was racist, 34–41,
54–62, 92
Railroads
coal shoveling, 23, 48
train jumping, 24–25, 48–49
Ranching
Bond family, 28
Judge Miller, 66, 113, 115
London, 23, 32–33, 129
wolf policy, 162–164
Reading
hobos, 48–49
London, 23, 26, 47
Realism
devolution, 98–101
fable/parable, 102–108
geography, 25
heroic quest, 77
naturalism, 12, 25
objectivity, 99
unrealistic depiction of animals, 105, 122–129, 130, 134
Rebirth stage of heroic quest, 75,
80, 81–83

The Red One (London) [collec-
tion], 32
"The Red One" (London) [short
story], 33
Reed, A. Paul, 87, 92
Reed, John, 37
Reesman, Jeanne Campbell, 75–84
Reforestation and wolf habitat,
156
Regan, Thomas (Hearts of Three),
128
Regression. See Atavism
Religion
Appalachia, 173–174, 175
isolation and God, 60
"The White Silence"
(London), 60
Reversion. See Atavism
Revolutionary fiction, 37
Ritual
adulthood, 118
apotheosis, 80
Spitz fight, 71, 119
The Road (London), 25, 106
Robisch, S.K., 130–139
Romances, 76–77
Romanticism, 37, 110, 111
Roosevelt, Theodore, 39, 44, 105,
125–126
Rossetti, Gina M., 85–93
Rothberg, Abraham, 14
Rousseau, Jean-Jacques, 63–68, 65
Russia and wolves, 137
See also Soviet Union and
London's popularity

S

Sacrifice, White Dog, 119
Sailing
oyster piracy, 9, 23, 26, 47

seal-hunting, 9, 10, 23, 26, 48

Snark (boat), 9–10, 30–32

Samoa, 32

San Francisco Chronicle, 123

San Francisco Examiner, 26, 48

A Sand County Almanac (Leopold), 158, 159

Sangster, Maud (*The Abysmal Brute*), 10–11

Santa Clara, CA, 28

Sartoris (Faulkner), 71

Satan (*Paradise Lost*), 147

The Scarlet Plague (London), 33, 38

Science fiction, London's, 34, 38

The Scorn of Women (London), 29

Scotch half-breed (*The Call of the Wild*), 114, 118

Scotland and wolves, 155

Scott, Wheedon (*White Fang*), 107

Scurvy, 9, 52

The Sea Wolf (London)

    fable/parable, 106

    German reaction, 38

    London's experiences seal-hunting, 26

    London's identification with wolves, 14, 128

    Moby-Dick (Melville), 119, 144–145

    myth, 136

    naturalism, 124

    quest for individualism, 140, 144–147

    rejection of civilization, 10

Seal-hunting, 9, 10, 23, 26, 48

    See also The Sea Wolf (London)

Self

    Campbell's stages of heroic quest, 75, 84

    determination, 173–174, 174

Sexuality

    Hemingway, Ernest, 57

    London, Jack, 58

    wildness, 170–171

Sheep wolf kills, 163

Siberian husky. *See* Huskies

Silence in wildness, 172

Simple living. *See* Pastoralism

Sinclair, Upton, 37

Sisk, John P., 69–70

Slavery, 174

Sled dog team. *See* Dog sled team

Sled pulling contest, 67, 82, 100

Sled team. *See* Dog sled team

Smith, Doug, 159

Smoke Bellew (London), 29

Smoking, 23

Snark (boat), 9–10, 23, 30–32

Snow bed

    absence of love, 116

    devolution, 12, 70, 96

Snowmobiles, 153

Snyder, Gary, 9, 71, 173

Socialism

    The Call of the Wild as a socialist folktale, 85–93

    critical reception, 56

    London's activities, 23, 34, 37–38, 49, 69, 102

    See also Capitalism, rejection

Society. *See* Civilization

Sol-leks (*The Call of the Wild*), 96, 114

"Soldier's Home" (Hemingway), 74

Solomon Islands, 32

"The Somnambulists" (London), 60, 124

A Son of the Sun (London), 32, 124

The Son of the Wolf: Tales of the Far North (London), 29, 101, 128

Song imagery, 78–80, 114, 132

Sophia Sutherland (ship). *See* Seal-hunting

South Sea Tales (London), 32

South Seas travel, 32

Soviet Union and London's popularity, 37, 38
    See also Russia and wolves

Spain
    bears, 160
    wolves, 156

Spencer, Herbert, 13, 123–124, 133, 138

Spitz (*The Call of the Wild*), 119
    alternative to working, 114–115
    anti-capitalism, 85, 86, 88
    Darwinism, 13–15
    devolution, 97–98
    father imagery, 118, 119
    lack of heroism, 71
    quest for individualism, 141
    whiteness, 118, 119

St. Vincent, Gregory (*A Daughter of the Snows*), 44, 45

Stealing
    Buck's rejection of civilization, 12
    capitalism, 85, 87–88
    devolution, 96
    London, 9, 23, 26, 47
    survival, 78, 96, 133

Steinbeck, John, 55

Steppenwolf (Hesse), 137–138

Sterling, George, 129

"The Story of Jees Uck" (London), 126

Strength
    atavism/ancestry, 106
    heroism, 102, 105
    individualism, 143, 145, 147
    myth, 105, 110
    The Sea-Wolf (London), 145, 147

"The Strength of the Strong" (London), 38, 105–106

Stroke, 33

Style
    mythic, 98–101
    objectivity, 99–100
    syntactical, 69, 73–74
    tone poetry, 78–80

Suicide
    Martin Eden (London), 10, 140, 148
    rumors of London's, 33

Sun imagery, 115

Supernatural
    ghost dog myth, 16, 68, 75, 83–84, 120
    stages of heroic quest, 82
    wolves, 137

Survival
    ancestral knowledge, 12–13, 70, 96–98
    Campbell's stages of heroic quest, 78
    freedom, 67
    morality, 14, 94, 123, 124–125, 133
    "To Build a Fire" (London), 23, 29

Sweden
    bears, 160
    moose, 163
    wolves, 156, 160, 163, 164

Switzerland and wolves, 156, 160
Symbolism
    heroic quest, 77, 80–81
    wolves, 137–138, 159, 162, 165
Syntactical style, 69, 73–74

T

Tagish Lake, 50
Tahiti, 32
Tales of the Fish Patrol (London),
    26
Tavernier-Courbin, Jacqueline, 15,
    94–101
Technology and alienation, 38
Television and disinterest in wil-
    derness, 150, 152
Tenderfeet. *See* Cheechakoes
30-Mile River, 50
Thoreau, Henry David, 69, 74,
    150, 152
Thornton, John (*The Call of the
    Wild*), 90
    Buck's rebirth, 82–83
    Buck's regression to tameness,
        98, 116, 142
    capitalism, 89–91
    death and freeing of Buck,
        15–16, 67, 83, 91, 99, 107,
        110
    family, 67, 118
    heroism, 101
    love, 67, 100, 107, 115, 116,
        142
    morality, 107
    nobility, 73
    work ethic, 113
"The Three Day Blow"
    (Hemingway), 16
"To Build a Fire" (London)
    autobiographical elements, 23,
        29

critical reception, 56, 103
    fable/parable, 105
    racism, 45
Tone poetry, 78–80
Tourism and wilderness, 150, 152–
    153
Trains
    coal shoveling, 23, 48
    jumping by London, 24–25,
        48–49
Tramping, 9, 23, 24–25, 48–49
Transcendence, 137
Transcendentalism, conflict with
    naturalism, 111
Transformation stage of heroic
    quest, 75, 76, 77–80
Transitory stage of development,
    64
Travels by Jack London
    Japan, 9, 26
    Pacific, 9, 32
    Snark, 9–10, 30–32
    tramping, 9, 23, 24–25, 48–49
    Yukon gold rush, 9, 14, 23,
        27–29, 46–52, *51*
Tree imagery in *Martin Eden*
    (London), 10
Trinity imagery, 73
Twain, Mark
    morality and survival, 124–
        125
    naturalism, 25
    rejection of civilization, 16,
        61, 69, 74, 109, 111–112

U

Unconscious
    appeal of *The Call of the Wild*,
        102, 105, 108
    Buck's journey, 13, 33, 84

Unemployment
   labor crisis and Buck's escape
    from capitalism, 85–93
   protests, 24, 47
United States
   American dream and wild-
    ness, 9, 70, 112
   disinterest in wilderness, 150–
    153
   freedom and integrity in Ap-
    palachia, 172–176
   wolves, 154–165
University of California, 27, 49
Unlearning, 11, 87
   See also Devolution; Educa-
    tion
"The Unparalleled Invasion"
   (London), 34, 40
Uremia, 33
US Fish and Wildlife Service, 162,
   164
US Forest Service, 158
Utah and wolves, 156

V

The Valley of the Moon (London),
   33
Van Weyden, Humphrey (*The Sea
   Wolf*), 10, 124, 141, 144–147
Versteeg, Desiree, 154–155
Video games, and lack of interest
   in wilderness, 150, 151–152
Vietnam War (1961-1975), 167

W

Wages, 47
Walcutt, Charles Child, 92
Walden (Thoreau), 69, 152
"The Waste Land" (Eliot), 55
"The Water Baby" (London), 33

Watson, Charles N., Jr., 109–121
Wellman, Flora, 25–26, 46, 47
Welse, Frona (*A Daughter of the
   Snows*), 29, 44
Wharton, Edith, 25
"When the World Was Young"
   (London), 38
Whipping boy, London as critics',
   54–62
White Dog sacrifice, 119
White Fang (London)
   autobiographical elements, 23,
    29
   critical reception, 56, 105
   fable/parable, 102, 106–108
   individualism, 140, 142–144
   insights from "Husky: The
    Wolf-Dog of the North"
    (London), 130–139
   London's identification with
    wolves, 128
   parallels with humans, 125
   realism/unrealism, 105, 127
"The White Silence" (London)
   Darwinism, 13–14
   isolation, 58–60
   whiteness, 117–118, 119, 136
White Steed of the Prairies (folk
   tale), 120
Whitehorse, YT, 35, 37, 41, 42
Whiteness and wildness, 109, 116,
   118–120, 136
Wilderness
   benefits of wildness, 166–171
   conservation, 39, 157–159
   disinterest, 150–153
   freedom and integrity, 172–
    176
   wolves and modern attitudes,
    154–165
Wildness
   American dream, 9, 70, 112

anti-capitalism, 85–93
benefits, 166–171, 172–176
devolution, 94–101
disinterest in wilderness, 150–153
fable/parable form, 102–108
freedom and integrity, 172–176
heroic quest, 75–84
"Husky: The Wolf-Dog of the North" (London), 130–139
individualism quest, 140–148
London's appeal, 54–62
London's Yukon trip, 9, 14, 27–29, 46–52, *51*
love's antithesis, 115
pastoralism, 69–74
racism, 34–41, 42–45
Rousseau's development of man, 63–68
Sea Wolf (London), 10, 124
vs. society, 109–121
unrealistic depiction of animals, 105, 122–129, 130, 134
Williamson, Eric Miles, 54–62
Winesburg, Ohio (Anderson), 70
Wit in fables, 103
The Wolf (Mech), 127
Wolf-dog. *See* Huskies
"Wolf House," 14, 23, 32–33, 129
"Wolf" nickname, 14, 129
Wolverines, 125
Wolves
    Buck compared to White Fang, 106
    Buck's leadership, 64, 67, 68, 83–84, 120, 130, 134
    family, 67, 68
    fear of humans, 127–128, 155
    hunting and conservation attitudes, 154–165
    huskies, 131–132

"The Law of Life," 126–127, 136
London's identification, 14, 128–129
morality, 130, 136
symbolism and mythology, 126, 137–138, 157, 159, 162, 165
unrealistic depictions, 105, 122, 125–128, 130, 134
See also White Fang (London)
Women, London portrayals, 42, 45, 54
"Wonder of Woman" (London), 118
Work
    London's jobs, 9, 23, 27, 46, 47–48
    pride, 112–113
    wildness as alternative, 114–115
World War I (1914-1918), 38
Wright, James, 71
Writing
    habits, 30–32, 33
    London's pursuit, 14, 25, 27, 46, 52
    London's subjects and genres, 23–24, 29
    Martin Eden (London), 10, 27
    San Francisco Examiner contest, 26, 48
    wildness and creative writing, 168, 169

X

Xenophobia, 40

Y

Yeehats
    displacement, 92

ghost dog myth, 16, 68, 75, 83–84, 120–121
killing by Buck, 68, 92, 99
killing of John Thornton, 15, 67, 83, 91, 99
"The Yellow Peril" (London), 56–57
Yellowstone National Park, 152, 159, 160, 161
Yukon gold rush, London's activities, 9, 14, 23, 27–29, 46–52, *51*

Yukon River, 28, 50–51
Yukon Territory
    Dawson City, 28, 51, *51*
    Whitehorse and allegations of London's racism, 35, 37, 41, 42

Z

Zaradic, Patricia, 151–153
Zola, Emile, 12, 110, 111

CPSIA information can be obtained
at www.ICGtesting.com
Printed in the USA
FFOW05n0110110414